THE LIFE, DEATH, AND RESURRECTION OF HARRY POTTER

MERCER
UNIVERSITY PRESS

Endowed by
TOM WATSON BROWN
and
THE WATSON-BROWN FOUNDATION, INC.

THE LIFE,
DEATH,
AND
RESURRECTION
OF
HARRY POTTER

John Killinger

MERCER UNIVERSITY PRESS

MACON, GEORGIA

MUP/P390

© 2009 Mercer University Press
1400 Coleman Avenue
Macon, Georgia 31207
All rights reserved

First Edition.

Books published by Mercer University Press are printed on acid free
paper that meets the requirements of American National Standard for
Information Sciences—Permanence of Paper for Printed Library
Materials.

Mercer University Press is a member of Green Press initiative
(greenpressinitiative.org), a nonprofit organization working to help
publishers and printers increase their use of recycled paper and decrease
their use of fiber derived from endangered forests. This book is printed
on recycled paper.
ISBN 13   978-0-88146-162-6

Library of Congress Cataloging-in-Publication Data

Killinger, John.
The life, death, and resurrection of Harry Potter / John Killinger. -- 1st
ed.
p. cm.
Includes bibliographical references and index.
ISBN-13: 978-0-88146-162-6 (pbk. : alk. paper)
ISBN-10: 0-88146-162-8 (pbk. : alk. paper)
1. Rowling, J. K.—Characters—Harry Potter. 2. Children's stories,
English—History and criticism. 3. Potter, Harry (Fictitious
character) 4. Children—Books and reading. 5. Rowling, J. K.—
Religion. 6. Christianity and literature. 7. Bible—In literature.
I. Title.
PR6068.O93Z7375 2009
823'.914--dc22
2009021722

This book is awe-fully and respectfully dedicated to J. K. Rowling, author of the Harry Potter novels, who I predict will one day be mentioned with Dante, Shakespeare, and Dickens in the quaternity of the world's greatest writers.

CONTENTS

INTRODUCTION

In *Harry Potter and the Deathly Hallows,* the seventh and final volume of J. K. Rowling's popular fictional series about the young wizard, Harry and his friend Hermione transport themselves—"Apparate"—to the small village of Godric's Hollow, where Harry's parents once lived and are now buried. Harry's youthful career as the fabled opponent of the evil Lord Voldemort is nearing its end. Had it not been for Voldemort, Harry ponders, he would have grown up in Godric's Hollow and returned there to spend school holidays with his parents.

Now, he and Hermione come to the town with a specific purpose. Having been in hiding for weeks, they are surprised to find that it's Christmas Eve. Then, as they cross the square toward the church to search for the graves of Harry's parents, Hermione exclaims, "Harry, look!"

> She was pointing at the war memorial. As they had passed it, it had transformed. Instead of an obelisk covered in names, there was a statue of three people: a man with untidy hair and glasses, a woman with long hair and a kind, prêtty face, and a baby boy sitting in his mother's arms. Snow lay upon all their heads, like fluffy white caps.[1]

Harry examines the statue closely, astonished to see himself as a happy baby with no scar on his forehead. After the two leave the statue and turn again toward the church, Harry looks back and sees that the memorial has returned to its regular form.

Rowling scatters clues all along, ever since the opening of the first volume, *Harry Potter and the Sorcerer's Stone*, when she introduces readers to Harry as an orphan being delivered to his aunt and uncle's home under extraordinary circumstances. When the baby arrives at the Dursleys', he is awaited by master wizard Dumbledore and his female consort Professor Minerva McGonagall and heralded by a downpour of shooting stars and thousands of owls flying everywhere in the daytime, confounding the national weather forecasters. Baby Harry also bears the mark of a lightning bolt on his forehead, left by Voldemort's death curse.

As I point out in my book *God, the Devil, and Harry Potter*, written after Rowling completed her fourth novel, the scar itself is a telltale sign, for not only is it the symbol of Zeus in Greek myths, but it also represents the unspeakable name of the Hebrew god Yahweh. Jews considered Yahweh's name so holy that their Scriptures identified it with the tetragram YHWH. It was pronounced only on Yom Kippur, and then solely on the lips of the high priest of Israel. According to legend, it was the name tendered to Moses when he asked the identity of the deity at the burning bush, and scholars believe it was originally the word that described a lightning flash—possibly the very lightning flash that set the bush afire.[2]

In the final volume of the Harry Potter saga, Rowling tips her hand completely: all along her young hero has been a Christ figure, the Messiah, doing battle with the Dark Lord, who is the embodiment of evil in the world. If most of the critics missed it in the earlier books—I believe I was alone in insisting on the identification—Rowling finally makes it unmistakable. Hermione and Harry visit

Godric's Hollow on Christmas Eve. Worshipers gather in the village church and sing carols. Suddenly, the war memorial in the center of the village, itself a symbol of humanity's age-old proneness to conflict and destruction, is transmogrified into a statue of the Holy Family—Mary, Joseph, and the Baby—or in this case Lily, James, and little Harry.

Rowling must have enjoyed the irony of knowing that hundreds, even thousands, of detractors all over the world attacked her books as wicked, evil, and anti-Christian because they glorified wizards and witches. Many believed the Harry Potter books represented the epitome of Satanic thought and behavior. Fundamentalists such as Reverend Jerry Falwell and spokespersons for Dr. James Dobson's Focus on the Family organization decried the novels as worldly, unchristian stories that condoned lying and deception and promoted witchcraft and demonism among their young, susceptible readers. Conservative critic Richard Abanes spoke for a host of irate Christian parents when he declared in *Harry Potter and the Bible* that Rowling's works were occult and New Age and clearly presented "far too much moral subjectivity and patently unbiblical actions to be of any ethical value."[3] Succumbing to this pressure, many librarians removed Rowling's books from their shelves, and those who didn't were often the target of wrath and calumny by community do-gooders. Some were fired for refusing to banish Harry Potter from their libraries.

But now it is all over. Rowling has revealed her secret: Harry is in fact a Christ figure in the order of other great Christ imitators of history—Melville's Billy Budd in *Billy Budd, Foretopman*; Dostoevsky's Prince Myshkin in *The Idiot*; Faulkner's Joe Christmas in *Light in August*; Kazantzakis's Manolios in *The Greek Passion*; and

Mauriac's Xavier Dartigelongue in *The Lamb*. Since the release of the final Potter book, an eerie quiet has descended upon the battle-field and there is surprisingly little discussion of the Potter saga. Why is that? Is it because the critics are embarrassed that they didn't see the truth before and come to Rowling's defense? Or is it that Harry's army of followers—millions of children, young people, and adults who anxiously awaited the publication of each highly touted volume of his exploits—are somehow disappointed to learn that Harry wasn't as unique as they believed? Is it possible that these readers now feel that Rowling cheated by having a template in mind when she formed Harry, one that has lain inextricably at the heart of all Western culture since the first century, when we began to mark the years by referring to the birth of a holy child who battled evil for the souls of all the people on earth?

Perhaps it is a little of each, and perhaps it doesn't matter. The suspense is over. Harry *does* die in the seventh volume, and, perhaps surprisingly to some readers, he also comes back to life, as Jesus did.

Well, not quite as Jesus did. Rowling must have debated with herself about how to end the story—whether to cut it off after the death, or, after bringing Harry back to engage in a final battle with Voldemort, to have him ascend into some kind of heaven the way Jesus supposedly did.

Personally, I suspect that her decision to give Harry an addi-tional span of life—of normal existence, actually, in which he marries Ginny Weasley and has children whom he and his wife dis-patch to Hogwarts for their formal education—may have been in-fluenced by Dan Brown's exceptionally popular *The Da Vinci Code*. Brown's novel prompted an outpouring of reaction to the suggestion that Jesus' widow and infant son escaped to France and speculation about whether the Savior of the world ever married and fathered children, as any rabbi of his time would surely have done.

As I say, it probably doesn't matter. Now Rowling's work belongs to posterity and the critics. It will be mined by hundreds, even thousands, of master's and Ph.D. students searching for acceptable thesis topics—"Ancient Legends in the Works of J. K. Rowling," "Mythological Animals in the Rowling Texts," "Symbolic Place Names in the Harry Potter Novels," "The Power of Love in J. K. Rowling," "The Relationship of Quidditch to Olympic Games through the Centuries," "New Insights into the Curriculum of Hogwarts and Their Application to Current Educational Theory," "The Popularity of Hagrid Figures in the Literature of Children," and, of course, "The Psychology of J. K. Rowling: Was Dumbledore Really Gay?" Such uses of popular stories are inevitable.

But it does matter that the record is set straight regarding Harry as a Christ figure—possibly the best known, most popular Christ figure of all time, one on whose actions and destiny hung the passionate attention of literally millions of children worldwide. At this time, the Potter novels approach 400 million copies sold, and they have been translated into more than 60 languages. Rowling's books have the most remarkable publishing record of all time, except perhaps for the Bible, the Qu'ran, the Bagavad-Gita, and a handful of other holy texts.

Psychologists may ponder whether the secret of Harry Potter's extraordinary popularity was not somehow inextricably tied up with readers' subliminal feelings for Jesus Christ. In a world where Jesus has always been the hero *par excellence*, the model human being, the epitome of selfless love and sacrifice, perhaps there was among Harry's followers some unidentified subconscious adoration of Christianity's Messiah. Jesus was, after all, both human and divine. Supposedly he was subject to all the temptations to which human flesh is heir—lust, greed, envy, and even hate—yet managed to rise above them to become the perfect sacrificial lamb, spotless and without blemish, for the salvation of the world.

What greater archetype could Rowling have chosen? Or perhaps she didn't choose it, and instead it chose her. That day on the train, as she sat for hours on the impeded journey to Manchester and outlined the story of Harry from beginning to end—she has often said that was the way it happened—did she become a witting or unwitting vessel for what Fulton Oursler once called "the greatest story ever told"? Was she chosen to rewrite the Christ saga as a story for modern readers, even as Joseph Girzone has rewritten it in his novels about Joshua, a contemporary carpenter from a small town in upstate New York? She will probably never say, of course, and possibly can't. Sometimes we are unaware of the great tidal urgings that ebb and flow beneath the surface of our unconscious—irresistible forces whose existence remains unknown to us even in the heat of creativity.

Many would agree that Rowling must be listed now among the world's great creative geniuses—the Dantes, Shakespeares, Mozarts, Tolstoys, Monets, and Picassos who, as they work, are seldom aware of the tremendous forces producing upheavals of generativity in the depths of their psyches. Few modern writers equal Rowling in the scope of her imagination or the cleverness with which she integrates ancient myth and modern storytelling. We can only guess at the unexpected sources of her talent and ability. What gave rise to such productivity in the life of a young woman essentially destitute when she began scribbling her works in a corner of a relative's café while drinking endless cups of coffee and occasionally jiggling her baby's pram to keep her quiet?

My guess—and in the end I must confess it is only a guess, for we are dealing here with essentially unquantifiable matters—is that J. K. Rowling, practically alone and friendless, accidentally or at the behest of fate tapped into the mother lode of all stories, the story of Christ, who was born in humble circumstances and grew up not only to battle evil but to become the most cited teacher in the history of humankind. Being schooled in legends and mythology by her training at Exeter University, Rowling retold that story—with embellishments—in a form she knew would appeal to every school child in her native England. Thus it was that the world read about an orphan boy who was reared in a hostile household by relatives who despised him, sent off to an otherworldly private school where he was educated among strange and often idiosyncratic professors, turned into an unlikely sports idol, and subjected to the same romantic dreams and disillusionments that afflict every teenage boy and girl.

When did it dawn on Rowling that she was rewriting the story of Christ? Maybe she knew it at the beginning when she outlined it all on the train. Or maybe it came later, when she began to notice the affinities between Harry and Jesus. Whenever it was, she made the most of it. She knew it would kill her story if she overplayed it and people recognized that she was writing about a known religious figure from the outset. The world is far too secular for that kind of Sunday school morality play. She had to be careful and subtle. Better portray Harry as an ordinary boy with a propensity for lying and deception. Show him as an occasional trickster, but don't overdo it, lest readers dismiss him as a mere Huck Finn or Dennis the Menace. Let Draco Malfoy be the villain in the story—a bully, a liar, and a coward. Harry simply had to be an all-around boy, one who lied in a pinch or pretended to think one thing and then did another. His friends too had to be average, though it must have been fun to make Hermione the smartest student in all her classes, the girl who left the boys in the dust when they were called on to recite wizarding history or produce arcane enchantments.

It probably helped Rowling that her conservative critics complained about Harry's mischievousness and occasional dishonesty. They played right into her hands. In her own mind, she knew that Jesus had been an ordinary boy too. She didn't buy all those myths about his never telling a lie and never having a bad thought cross his mind—the stuff of pious medieval legends. But making Harry such a real boy diverted her audience. She wrote about the Savior of the world and nobody knew it.

Well, almost nobody.

I have to admit at the outset that I'm writing this book to crow a little. Not objectionably, I hope. I did hold my breath as I turned the pages of the final volume in Rowling's series. What if Harry didn't die? What if he engaged in a last battle with Voldemort and dispatched him as easily as Superman dealt with Lothar or Batman overcame the Joker? That was a possibility. After all, few had joined me as part of a chorus proclaiming Harry's similarity to Jesus. Maybe I was wrong and would have to slink away and say nothing.

Thankfully, I wasn't wrong. I say thankfully because I can imagine my disappointment if Harry had not been a Christ figure. It would have left him a mere secular hero, popular in the hearts and minds of millions of children but somehow reduced in stature to the ranks of a comic book character or a matinee idol from some popular film series.

As it is, he participates in the greatest saga of all history. He is a successful embodiment of the central myth of Western culture. For millions of readers, he epitomizes that myth, both feeds and is fed by it, and thereby enjoys a oneness with it that elevates him above mere literary eminence into the realm of immortality. We cannot examine Harry apart from the story of Jesus; and, if the story of Jesus is fully told, it must now include an examination of the story of Harry Potter, for Harry mystically embodies and extends that story.

Hence this book is essentially a review of the ways Harry and his friends remind us of Jesus and his disciples, and an exploration of how Harry, like Jesus, was called literally from his birth—or at least from his earliest encounter with Voldemort—to engage in a fateful battle with evil and overcome it, thereby offering hope and encouragement to all who knew and admired him. This book breaks little fresh ground, for its message is already told. But the following is a necessary—indeed, an obligatory—recovering of the ground of the Harry Potter novels to observe the way Rowling strewed it with clues that identify Harry's story with Jesus', so that we have a fuller understanding of the sheer artistry of the woman who may well be the greatest storyteller of all time.

1

A World Divided

It is a classic mark of the West's great religions, from Zoroastrianism on, that they all see the world as inextricably caught in a death struggle between good and evil. This wasn't true of the Greeks and Romans, who believed reason and moderation could usually subdue evil. But Persians, Egyptians, Hebrews, and Christians have always had a strong belief in the ultimate duality of life that forever threatens to destroy any human beings who don't unreservedly ally themselves with the forces of good.

This belief is basic to all great Western literature, providing the natural dramatic tension of such works as *Beowulf, The Divine Comedy, The Faerie Queene*, all of Shakespeare's tragedies, *Paradise Lost* and *Paradise Regained, Moby-Dick, Oliver Twist*, and *The Brothers Karamazov*. It has also been the foundation of modern crime and detective stories, science fiction, and the fantasy writings of the great Oxford dons C. S. Lewis, J. R. R. Tolkien, and Charles Williams, who, together with Charles Dickens, are the most obvious forerunners of the novels of J. K. Rowling.

In her first novel, *Harry Potter and the Sorcerer's Stone* (*The Philosopher's Stone* in England), Rowling wastes no time exposing the enormous and often disastrous friction in Harry's world between good and evil. Harry's parents, James and Lily Potter, have been killed in an encounter with Lord Voldemort, the malevolent ruler of the Dark Arts, and Voldemort has attempted to destroy baby Harry with an *Avada Kedavra* curse, or killing spell. Fortunately for Harry—and for the entire wizard world he is chosen to champion—the spell rebounds upon Voldemort himself, almost annihilating him, and leaves Harry with a lightning-shaped scar on his forehead that later tingles and even burns to warn Harry of the approach of evil.

Voldemort's name is dark and menacing. It reminds us of Vortigern, the evil king in the Arthurian legends who schemed to murder Merlin. Rowling's intended meaning is not completely certain, but the name probably signifies either "flight of death" (from the French *voler*, "to fly") or "will of death" (from the Latin *volo*, "to will" or "to be willing"). Either way, it is evocative of shadows, threats, and scheming, and easily sets the stage for the epic contest that occupies Rowling's talents for seven long volumes of narration.

Perhaps the openness with which Rowling presents her theme at the beginning of the septet is what some critics find so disturbing about exposing children to her writings. However, Rowling has defended herself on this point in numerous interviews, contending that children not only can withstand such straight talk about good and evil but also are well served when introduced to the duality as an integral part of their indoctrination into the harsher realities of human existence.

Maria Tatar, Loeb professor of Germanic languages and literature at Harvard, has made a career of writing about the dark side of such fairy tales as "Bluebeard," "Little Red Riding Hood," and

"Hansel and Gretel." The "once-upon-a-timeness" of these stories makes them safe for children to read, she says, and actually helps them to be less afraid of the threats and difficulties they encounter in life. The important thing about J. K. Rowling, Tatar contends, is that she "writes *for* children but never *down* to them." She never shies away from "the great existential mysteries: death and loss, cruelty and compassion, desire and depression. Think of those fiendish Dementors who are experts in making you lose hope— what could be more frightening than that?" But Rowling doesn't abandon her readers to such frightening creatures. She actually puts magic into their hands—"they are the anointed and the appointed," says Tatar. Reading the Harry Potter stories, children actually feel *commissioned* to struggle against such debilitating threats.[4]

From the opening pages of *The Sorcerer's Stone*, readers are comforted by the knowledge that Harry's arrival at the home of his Muggle (non-magical) aunt and uncle, the Dursleys of number 4 Privet Drive, is special. Strange things happen all over the country to signal it: weird-looking people walk around in bright-colored cloaks; owls swoop about in broad daylight; perfect strangers hug one other for no reason at all; and that night two unusual figures arrive at the Dursley home—Albus Dumbledore, tall and thin with silvery hair and a beard long enough to tuck into his belt, and Professor Minerva McGonagall, appearing in the form of a cat. The two exchange greetings and McGonagall mentions that she has been sitting there all day, watching the Dursley home. "All day?" Dumbledore says. "When you could have been celebrating? I must have passed a dozen feasts and parties on the way here."[5]

There's the clue: Harry's arrival was a time of celebration. Those who knew who he was—the boy wizard who would save them all from the evil Lord Voldemort—were elated at his coming, just as the faithful souls of Israel were reportedly elated at the coming of Christ. The whole wizard world buzzed with the news of Harry's survival of his initial encounter with Voldemort, and there were parties galore in anticipation of his growing up to defeat Voldemort definitively, once and for all.

Of course, most Israelites were completely unaware of the birth of Christ, and the early church fabricated stories to make it appear that many people knew about it and celebrated. Specifically, the Gospels of Matthew and Luke created such stories. Mark, which most scholars consider the earliest Gospel, offers no such tales; and John, undoubtedly the last of the four Gospels, foregoes any reference to the infant Christ to speak instead of a transcendent, preexistent Christ: "In the beginning was the Word, and the Word was with God, and the Word was God" (John 1:1). Matthew writes about the wise men from the East who journeyed to Jerusalem in search of the special child who had been born (Matt 2:1–12), and Luke bequeaths us the lovely stories of Mary and her cousin Elizabeth, the shepherds visited by angels, and the two elderly persons in the temple, Simeon and Anna, who rejoiced at seeing the baby Messiah (Luke 1:26–55; 2:8–20; 2:21–38).

The first pages of the Harry Potter saga offer a flavor of the Matthean story of the so-called Massacre of the Innocents, when Herod sought the deaths of all male children in Israel under the age of two years in order to eliminate the Christ child. Lord Voldemort has similarly sought to slay the child whose coming threatens him, but has failed. Harry, bearing the fresh lightning scar on his forehead, is spirited into hiding with his Muggle relatives, just as, according to the Gospel of Matthew, the baby Jesus was hustled into Egypt by his father and mother to avoid the power of King Herod.

The Two Dumbledores?

Dumbledore, as I suggest in *God, the Devil, and Harry Potter,* may well stand for God the Father in the novels, for, while he isn't actually Harry's father, as God was not Jesus' earthly father, he becomes his primary mentor and spiritual father in the stories. We shouldn't be put off by Rowling's comment to a young boy in an interview at Carnegie Hall[6] that Dumbledore was gay. She has never been given to truly inadvertent comments on her stories and characters, and it is likely that this was an intentional "slip," perhaps to confuse her audience and keep them guessing about the real nature of the great Hogwarts headmaster.

In the early days of space travel, many people joked about the astronauts' discovery that God and heaven were not precisely as orthodox Christians had always imagined them to be. One joke concerned an astronaut who comes back from a visit to heaven and says he has good news and bad news. The good news is that God exists in spite of all the bad press about the deity. The bad news is that *she* is really pissed off! Rowling, I suspect, was taunting us about Dumbledore in much the same manner. Wouldn't it be something if God were really gay?

Is Dumbledore gay? Psychologists emphasize the difference between being homosexual and being homoerotic, and the relationship Rowling describes between Dumbledore and his boyhood friend Gellert Grindelwald—who is proclaimed by Rita Skeeter in her muckraking biography *The Life and Lies of Albus Dumbledore* one of the "Most Dangerous Dark Wizards of All Time," next to

Voldemort himself—is clearly of the latter nature. The two were co-conspirators in the early days, plotting to seize power over the Muggle world, and Dumbledore was intoxicated, as many young men in his situation would have been, by their closeness and dreams. Consider William Wordsworth and Samuel Taylor Coleridge ambling through the English Lake District while planning *The Lyrical Ballads* and their impending revolution in poetry.

"Grindelwald," Dumbledore says to Harry in the heavenly interlude between Harry's final encounters with Voldemort. "You cannot imagine how his ideas caught me, Harry, inflamed me. Muggles forced into subservience. We wizards triumphant. Grindelwald and I, the glorious young leaders of the revolution."[7]

Dumbledore explains that the two men sought three objects—the Deathly Hallows—whose union would give them invincible power over everything. One was the Elder Wand, an unbeatable weapon. Another was the Resurrection Stone, which enabled its owner to recall loved ones from the grave. The third was the Invisibility Cloak, which Harry has actually inherited from his father, James. Dumbledore says his greatest desire was for the Resurrection Stone, so that he could bring back his deceased parents, relieving him of responsibility for his brother Aberforth and his sister Ariana. In the end, he and Grindelwald fought, and Ariana was killed by a flying curse during the fight. Nobody ever knew who spoke the curse, and Dumbledore blames himself. Grindelwald fled to the continent, and the two men didn't see each other for years.

Later, as a mature wizard, Dumbledore was offered the post of Minister of Magic, the greatest honor in the wizarding world—not once, but several times. Each time he refused, because he says he learned that he was not to be trusted with such power. Instead, he discovered the importance of love and service.

Dumbledore dies in volume six, *Harry Potter and the Half-Blood Prince*, so of course he cannot have truly represented God the Father to Harry *qua* Christ. Or could he? Rowling has a tricky mind. She loves to play with ideas, arranging and rearranging possibilities. Yet, suppose young Albus Dumbledore and young Gellert Grindelwald are God the Father and the Archangel Satan, collaborating on plans for the world. Satan was the Angel of Light, the one closest to God the Father. Then they fell out, and God the Father had to expel Satan from heaven. John Milton majestically describes this event in *Paradise Lost*:

> Him the almighty power
> Hurled headlong flaming from the ethereal sky
> With hideous ruin and combustion down
> To bottomless perdition, there to dwell
> In adamantine chains and penal fire,
> Who durst defy the omnipotent to arms.
> Nine times the space that measures day and night
> To mortal men, he with his horrid crew
> Lay vanquished, rolling in the fiery gulf
> Confounded though immortal.[8]

It is all myth and imagination, of course. The Second Epistle of Peter includes a brief reference to the fall of Satan and the angels—"If God did not spare the angels when they sinned, but cast them into hell and committed them to chains of deepest darkness to be kept until the judgment..." (2 Pet 2:4)—but nothing more substantial exists outside of legend and folklore. The story is part of an ancient people's attempt to explain the origin of the great contest between good and evil in the world. At first God and the devil were like twins, both on the same side. Then they had a falling out, and God expelled the devil and his followers from heavenly places. From then on, they have been at war. The book of Job, probably the oldest piece of literature in the entire Bible, describes Satan as "going to and fro on the earth" and "walking up and down on it" (Job 2:2), looking for those he can tempt and bend to his ways. In the biblical book, Satan persuades God to let him put Job to the test, to see if Job will desert God when besieged by troubles. The two of them—God and the devil—fight endlessly for the souls of people.

Consider further the possibility that young Albus Dumbledore was the God of the Old Testament, to whom power and control were everything, and the mature Albus Dumbledore was the God of the New Testament, a kindly father who now cared only for love and forgiveness and restoration. In this latter position, Dumbledore counsels Harry that he must go back to earth to face Voldemort for a second time.

But what about Dumbledore's death in *The Half-Blood Prince?* If he represents God the Father, could he have died? Why not? *Time* magazine boldly announced on one of its covers—the Easter issue on April 8, 1966—that "God Is Dead." Nietzsche had proclaimed as much a century earlier in *Thus Spake Zarathustra.* Now, according to *Time* magazine, a number of modern theologians, including Thomas J. J. Altizer and William Hamilton, were saying that the God of the Judeo-Christian religion was effectively deceased and it was time to bury him. J. K. Rowling probably wasn't born yet and didn't see that issue. But did she hear or read about it later? Regardless, the possibility of God's death has been the subject of considerable discussion in the Christian world for a number of years.

In *The Half-Blood Prince*, Dumbledore's funeral, attended by "an extraordinary assortment of people" from the wizarding world—"shabby and smart, old and young"—is worthy of a god. It is held out of doors, down by the lake, and next to a marble catafalque. An eerie musical lament sung by a chorus of merpeople fills the air. "It spoke very clearly of loss and despair."[9] The immense, sorrowing Hagrid carries the body, "wrapped in purple velvet spangled with golden stars," to the catafalque and then returns to sit beside his half-brother, the giant Grawp, "his great ugly boulder-like head bowed, docile, almost human." The merpeople, whom we first meet in *The Goblet of Fire*, draw near under the water and offer their own "strange, otherworldly music," and when a "tufty-haired" little man in black robes gives a short eulogy, they break the surface of the water to listen too. Across the lake, centaurs stand among the trees to pay their respects.[10]

Suddenly people scream as white flames erupt around the catafalque, leaping upwards until they obscure the body. The white smoke spiraling above the flames forms strange shapes, and Harry thinks he sees a phoenix flying joyfully into the blue sky above. Then the flames suddenly die out, and in their place stands a white marble tomb, encasing Dumbledore's body and the catafalque on which it rests. A shower of arrows swishes through the air as the centaurs' final tribute to Dumbledore. Then the creatures turn and disappear into the forest. The merpeople too sink from view, returning to their city beneath the water.[11]

Harry remembers Dumbledore's words, that it is important "to fight, and fight again, and keep fighting, for only then could evil be kept at bay, though never quite eradicated."[12] He tells his girlfriend Ginny Weasley that he cannot be with her anymore: "It's been like…like something out of someone else's life, these last few weeks with you," he says. "But I can't…we can't…I've got things to do alone now."[13]

He is now alone the way Christ was alone when he went to the cross. Harry would see Dumbledore again—only not in this life. "I know that you were very close to Dumbledore," Rufus Scrimgeour, the Minister of Magic, later confides to Harry. "I think you may have been his favorite pupil ever. The bond between the two of you…."[14]

The whole saga is very Christological, about Harry/Dumbledore and Jesus/God the Father. And it is about love versus the power of evil. In the end, Harry must become the sacrificial lamb and go to Dumbledore in the life beyond this one. Finally, he has to return from the grave to defeat Voldemort in a definitive way.

The Holy Spirit and Christian Concepts of Evil

Harry's defeat of Voldemort is the eventual denouement signaled from the opening of book one, *The Sorcerer's Stone,* and the entire series is an extended commentary on the great struggle at the heart of all human existence, the apparently never-ending battle between good and evil. This battle gives the first volume immediate pertinence to readers' lives, even the children, and it undergirds each successive volume.

We know that the story is important—or at least *sense* that it is—because it is the basic story of all Western religions. It is a recasting of humanity's ancient and timeless effort to overcome evil and self-destructiveness in its bid for survival, and it thoughtfully and creatively follows the plot of the Christian narrative about Jesus, a child of obscurity whose existence aroused the fearful enmity of evildoers and who grew up to be the champion of true righteousness the people expected him to be.

The sense of evil in all the Potter stories is palpable, and it strongly underlies the tales about wizards and witches that repel conservative critics who object to their presence. Maybe younger children shouldn't be exposed to such blatant personifications of wickedness as they meet in Rowling's books; parents must make that judgment for their own children. But Rowling herself is convinced that children can handle the confrontation. In various interviews, she says that her own encounter with villains in the books she read as a child strengthened her sense of right and wrong without making her afraid of the darker elements in the world.

Professor Tatar agrees with Rowling, whose enormous success, she thinks, owes a great deal to the brilliance with which Rowling taps into rich literary traditions such as fairy tales, ancient myths and legends, the writings of Dickens, and the omniprevalent horror films of our time. "She is the master of *bricolage*," says Tatar, "recycling stories and stitching them together in vibrant new ways. Rowling is on record as declaring her favorite author to be Jane Austen, but in the *Harry Potter* books there is also much of Dickens and [Roald] Dahl, with heavy doses of fairy tales and Arthurian legend, British boarding-school books, and murder mysteries. We have all the archetypal themes and characters of children's literature: an abject orphan, toxic stepparents, false heroes, helpers and donors, villainy and revenge."[15]

Religious conservatives, if they wish to cavil about children's exposure to the deepest existential themes in Rowling's saga, should consider what some children hear and learn in their own churches from Sunday school teachers and ministers eager to save them from everlasting damnation: descriptions of souls suffering in the flames of hell, warnings about the allure of the devil in innumerable tempting disguises, and threats that they can be lost for eternity because of mere thoughts of sexuality or a single instance of taking the Lord's name in vain. At least, in Rowling's works, children are provided with a sense of empowerment through Harry and his cohorts, themselves mere children who learn through their education at Hogwarts to resist evil in its many forms and arm themselves with knowledge and linguistic skills for the inevitable battles they will face as adults.

For more than two decades, one of the local topics of conversation in Lynchburg, Virginia, site of the late Reverend Jerry Falwell's Thomas Road Baptist Church (TRBC) and Liberty University, has been TRBC's "Scare Mare," an annual Halloween experience that is a cross between Disney World and a Bella Lugosi horror film. Manned by students from TRBC and Liberty University, it offers a gamut of frightening encounters with ghosts, witches, and evil monsters designed to "literally scare the hell out of kids," as one local observer put it, before sitting them down for a hard-sell lecture on sin and salvation and inviting them to accept Christ as their Savior. This is from the same people who campaigned against children reading the Harry Potter stories on the grounds that the books are filled with witches and wizards and confrontations with an adult variety of evils.

Rowling never makes the evil and wickedness in her stories attractive to children. On the contrary, it is invariably shown for what it is, a selfish preoccupation with personal gain and power. Draco Malfoy and his friends Crabbe and Goyle are never viewed as likable except to their own kind, who are all members of the House of Slytherin. The name Slytherin, with its subtle ability to conjure up images of snakes and sliminess, stands in contrast with the names of the other houses, Gryffindor, Hufflepuff, and Ravenclaw. Lord Voldemort himself, the prince of darkness in these stories, becomes more and more snakelike, hissing in Parseltongue (snake language), and keeps as his precious pet a repulsive, twelve-foot-long serpent named Nagini.

As in real life, good and evil in Rowling's narratives appear to expand and contract from season to season, first one and then the other gaining ascendancy. In the first of the novels, Voldemort's power is greatly diminished and curtailed by his failed attempt to murder the infant Harry Potter. By the fourth volume, *Harry Potter and the Goblet of Fire*, his power gradually returns, thanks to the ministries of his various followers in the government and on the faculty at Hogwarts. By volume six, *The Half-Blood Prince*, Voldemort appears to be at full tide again, for in this book Draco Malfoy and his friends exert their strongest influence at Hogwarts and Dumbledore is eventually killed. This, of course, sets the stage for the seventh and final volume, *The Deathly Hallows*, in which Harry Potter himself dies at Voldemort's hands, but then comes back to deal him a fatal blow.

Rowling conveys a message about the nature of evil that is essentially what we find in the New Testament: evil is insidious and omnipresent and all but ineradicable. Her message follows precisely, in fact, the description Jesus gives in the Gospel of Matthew when he tells a parable to his listeners:

Weeds and wheat

The kingdom of heaven may be compared to someone who sowed good seed in his field; but while everybody was asleep, an enemy came and sowed weeds among the wheat, and then went away. So when the plants came up and bore grain, then the weeds appeared as well. And the slaves of the householder came and said to him, 'Master, did you not sow good seed in your field? Where, then, did these weeds come from?' He answered, 'An enemy has done this.' The slaves said to him, 'Then do you want us to go and gather them?' But he replied, 'No; for in gathering the weeds you would uproot the wheat along with them. Let both of them grow together until the harvest; and at harvest time I will tell the reapers, Collect the weeds first and bind them in bundles to be burned, but gather the wheat into my barn.'" (Matt 13:24–30)

Snape & Dumbledore

Dumbledore understands that good and evil are often inseparable, and as a result seems unexpectedly tolerant of the sins and inadequacies of others. Harry and his friends wonder why he trusts Severus Snape, head of the House of Slytherin and once known to be a disciple of Voldemort. Dumbledore cannot tell them at the time—it is something they must eventually learn for themselves—but he sees both the mixed nature of good and evil in the world and the ability of those who have erred to repent and perform good acts. Snape actually kills Dumbledore at the end of book six, *The Half-Blood Prince* (he himself *is* the half-blood prince), but it is an action to which Dumbledore previously bound him. Knowing he is dying, Dumbledore wants it to appear that Snape is doing Voldemort's bidding.

Snape himself certainly understands the protean nature of evil. As he warns his students in Defense Against the Dark Arts class, "The Dark Arts…are many, varied, ever-changing, and eternal. Fighting them is like fighting a many-headed monster, which, each time a neck is severed, sprouts a head even fiercer and cleverer than before. You are fighting that which is unfixed, mutating, indestructible."[16]

Harry himself is not entirely pure—perhaps a reflection of Rowling's notion that Christ, as a human being, was not without sin and error—because he is an unwitting Horcrux for Voldemort. A Horcrux, which Professor Slughorn earlier told young Tom Riddle (who grew into Voldemort) is "the supreme act of evil" because it involves murdering someone and having one's own soul split apart,[17] is a depository for part of one's soul so that if the other part dies, the part in the Horcrux will survive. *Horcrux*

Just as Dumbledore was greedy for power as a young man, Harry Potter also carries part of Voldemort's nature in him. This is Rowling's opinion on good and evil: they are not totally separable in this life. The bad have a little good in them—even Voldemort did in his earlier days—and the good have a little bad in them. *We all have good and bad. Firefite*

Is this opinion theologically indefensible? Not at all. It is, in fact, the kind of admixture to which most religions agree, at least between the lines. Zeus and Jupiter, in the Greek and Roman pantheons, were both flawed divinities with humanlike lusts and enmities. Hinduism's Shiva, the deity who is the model for self-renunciation, is also characterized by radically antisocial behavior: fond of hallucinogens, he dances with goblins and fiends in *Shiva* cremation grounds and wanders naked through the cosmic regions. Even Judaism, with its august picture of Yahweh's righteousness and moral loftiness, confesses to his jealousy and unbridled appetite for command and power. He often changes his mind. He becomes angry with the people he professes to love. In the book of Hosea, he even sounds downright petty: "Since you have forgotten the law of your God, I also will forget your children" (Hos 4:6).

In the Potter series, Rowling, who is handily conversant with a wide background of folklore and religions, does not feel compelled to subscribe to the pious characterization of God preferred by many church and temple goers. Instead, she deals as whimsically and creatively with her portraits of God the Father and Jesus the Son as she does with all the other characters in her books. But we must not dismiss the analogies on this basis. There is convincing evidence that she had both God and Christ in mind when crafting Dumbledore and Harry.

There is even a strong likelihood, as I point out in *God, the Devil, and Harry Potter*, that Rowling fancied certain imagistic ties between the third person of the Christian trinity, the Holy Spirit, and Dumbledore's phoenix Fawkes. Fawkes's name is suggestive: Guy Fawkes was part of the famous Gunpowder Plot to blow up the king, lords, and commons when Parliament assembled on November 5, 1605. Many rebels were involved, but Fawkes, who guarded the powder, was the most famous one to be seized, taken to the tower, and hanged. November 5 became Guy Fawkes Day, and every year his effigy is burned and fireworks are shot off in hundreds of locations all over England.

In the case of Dumbledore's phoenix, Fawkes is a majestic, swan-sized bird with crimson feathers, a glittering golden tail as long as a peacock's, and gleaming golden talons. In *Harry Potter and the Chamber of Secrets,* Fawkes rescues Harry when he is at the mercy of the memory of Tom Riddle—a.k.a. Lord Voldemort— and a fierce basilisk that comes to life out of a statue of Salazar Slytherin, founder of the Slytherin House. When Tom refers to himself as "the greatest sorcerer in the world,"[18] Harry responds, "You're not...the greatest sorcerer in the world.... Sorry to disappoint you and all that, but the greatest wizard in the world is Albus Dumbledore."[19] Immediately upon expressing this loyalty to Dumbledore, Harry hears an eerie and powerful music that ends with an eruption of flames. It is the phoenix, Fawkes, who drops the school Sorting Hat (which assigns each student to a particular house) at Harry's feet.

Riddle calls a gigantic basilisk to kill Harry, but Fawkes blinds the great snake by gouging out its eyes. The basilisk still charges him, and, desperate, Harry remembers that the Sorting Hat contains the sword of Godric Gryfindor. Plunging the sword into the snake's mouth, Harry fatally wounds it, but a fang from the snake pierces Harry's arm and causes him to fade into unconsciousness. Fawkes helps him again, crying healing tears into the wound until Harry's strength returns and he can stab Riddle's diary, through which Voldemort has tormented the school, with the basilisk's fang, effectively destroying one of the seven Horcruxes. Fawkes aids Harry once more, carrying him and his friends up and out of the Chamber of Secrets to safety.[20] Later, Dumbledore thanks Harry as the two of them sit in front of the fire in his office. "You must have shown me real loyalty down in the Chamber," he says. "Nothing but that could have called Fawkes to you."[21]

Is it too much to say that Fawkes is a symbol or representation of the Holy Spirit in Christian theology? In the Gospels, the Spirit often comes to Jesus' aid when he is tempted or in need. In the book of Acts, Luke describes the coming of the Spirit on the crowd gathered at Pentecost: "Suddenly from heaven there came a sound like the rush of a violent wind, and it filled the entire house where they were sitting. Divided tongues, as of fire, appeared among them, and a tongue rested on each of them. All of them were filled with the Holy Spirit and began to speak in other languages, as the Spirit gave them ability" (Acts 2:2–4).

The tongues of fire, or licking flames, have long been associated with the Spirit and are a prominent feature in many churches' logos and decorative arts even today. In medieval bestiaries and illuminated manuscripts, the Spirit is often represented by the figure of a bird in crimson and gold.

Fawkes appears to mourn deeply when Dumbledore dies in book six. But then there is a strange description of white smoke curling up from the bier where the flames lick around Dumbledore's body. Harry thinks he sees a phoenix "fly joyfully into the blue."[22] Was it an idle remark on the author's part, or did she intend to suggest that Dumbledore's phoenix, as phoenixes have always been wont to do, rose triumphantly from his ashes?

The Basic Plan

Here then is what I propose as the basic plan of Rowling's entire series of Potter stories. She is dealing with nothing less than the plot of Christianity—the dividedness of the world between God and Satan, the coming of a lonely human figure who would bear the brunt of evil's curse in his own body, and the Holy Spirit of God that watched over him and encouraged him in his darkest hours.

Perhaps she saw it all in a flash as she began dreaming about Harry Potter that day on the train to Manchester. Why not write an epic story about the entire Christian myth, only make a strange, orphaned boy the central character—the Christ figure—who would gradually come to understand his mission in life, which was to destroy the evil figure who attacked him in his infancy? It would mean giving him close friends or disciples, having him learn to deal with the threat of evil when he went to school, and eventually pitting him mano a mano against the evil character in a battle he could not possibly win. It would have to be a sacrificial death. Then, in order to follow the Christ story to the letter, he would have to be resurrected.

My guess is that Rowling was uncertain about what to do after that—whether to end the final book on the triumphal note of the resurrection or to provide Harry and his friends with a normal life in a world without Voldemort—and that she was strongly influenced, when the time came, by the trend in biblical literature and modern fiction to question the business of the resurrection and what happened to the people closest to Jesus after it occurred. There were probably debates with her editors at Bloomsbury and Scholastic, as well as with her agent and maybe even her husband, about how to handle the ending of the saga, and she probably knew she was taking a genuine risk for the whole series when she created the brief epilogue at the end of book seven.

The question raised in my mind by the enormous commercial success of the entire enterprise—millions of copies sold in more than five dozen languages—is how readers will react now that it is over and they have a chance to digest what happened. More particularly, I am interested in how they react to the news that Ms. Rowling was writing a mammoth *Christian* fable all along. Does that take away some of the magic? Surely it doesn't diminish the sheer fun of the books—the witticisms and practical jokes and schoolyard pranks—or the cleverness with which Rowling has woven together bits and pieces of a number of the world's great myths and fairy tales. But to realize that she was following a pattern, that of the Christian Gospels themselves, so that there was no chance from the beginning that Harry Potter might overcome Lord Voldemort and his followers without having to die in the process, but *must inevitably die a horrible death*, may for some readers weaken their respect for Rowling's inventiveness, considerable as it was.

I would also like to know how the news affects Rowling's more acerbic critics—all those conservative and fundamentalist Christians who inveighed against the books on the grounds that they made witchcraft too attractive for impressionable young minds and glorified lying and trickery in their youthful hero and his friends. Will they suddenly gain a new respect for the Potter narratives, or will they resent the usage Rowling has made of their most sacred story in crafting a highly commercial retelling of it? The latter, I expect. But I would be pleased if it were otherwise.

"Imitation," as the English writer Caleb Charles Colton once said, "is the sincerest form of flattery." For J. K. Rowling, a young woman acquainted with the church and its story in the same way that every Englishman or Englishwoman knows about it, partly by osmosis and partly by a certain amount of reading and practice, to have chosen to pattern her lengthy saga of Harry Potter on the glorious narrative at the heart of the Christian faith is a compliment beyond any other she could have paid it. Perhaps the finest compliment for her as a creative artist is that she managed for so long and through so many pages to disguise what she was doing, leaving all of her critics in almost total darkness until the end of the tale.

Even then, I believe, she worried that the world had become so far gone in Potter mania that readers might fail to recognize the pattern she was following, so that she must leave stronger and stronger clues to shock them into the realization that she was actually writing about a familiar theme, the salvation of the world through Jesus Christ. Thus, in the final book we get not only a number of smaller clues but the blockbuster revelations of the metamorphosing war memorial scene, Harry Potter's willing embrace of death at the hands of Voldemort, his meeting with Dumbledore in a paradisial setting after death, and his return to life to put a definitive end to the Dark Lord's evil career.

Whatever the truth of all this, Rowling's is a monumental achievement: the most avidly followed and closely scrutinized treatment of the Passion Story in all history!

2

Harry and His Disciples

"Now about eight days after these sayings Jesus took with him Peter and John and James, and went up on the mountain to pray" (Luke 9:29). This occasion in the Gospel of Luke, followed by the story of the transfiguration of Christ, occurs near the end of Jesus' ministry. In earlier references to the calling of the disciples, Jesus first selected *four* disciples—the brothers Peter and Andrew and the brothers James and John—but Andrew does not figure prominently in the Gospel stories, and popular imagination almost always remembers *three* of the Apostles who were actually close to Jesus and therefore regularly accompanied him. Of these, of course, Simon Peter was undoubtedly closest to him, and Jesus reportedly established him as the first bishop of the Church.

A disciple—from the Greek word for "learner"—was officially a person who followed another for the purpose of hearing his teachings and generally learning to pattern his life after him. Jesus' disciples were also known as apostles, from the Greek word meaning "to send"; he sent them out to preach the message of the kingdom of God and make more disciples.

In the Harry Potter series, because Harry is himself still a student—he attends Hogwarts, the main wizarding school in Britain—his friends Ronald Weasley, Hermione Granger, and Neville Longbottom can hardly be styled "disciples." But they do form a friendship band around young Potter that eventually resembles that of the disciples around Jesus. Their friendship is tested again and again in the novels but never truly broken.

When Harry, Ron, and Hermione visit eccentric Xenophilus Lovegood's house in *The Deathly Hallows*, Harry climbs the stairs to his friend Luna Lovegood's room. As he mounts the stairs, he notices something remarkable. Luna has decorated her bedroom ceiling with portraits of Harry, Ron, Hermione, Neville, and Ron's sister Ginny—Harry's girlfriend—and has created delicate golden chains around the pictures, binding them all together. When Harry gets further up the steps and examines the chains more closely, he realizes they are formed by a single word, repeated a thousand times in golden ink: *friends…friends… friends….*[23]

At one level, the relationship is that of ordinary school chums drawn to one another by the fact that they are all in the same house—Gryffindor—and have a natural bond as members of the same competitive group. The various houses at Hogwarts receive or lose points according to the accomplishments or offenses of its members. For example, a master may impulsively grant ten points to Hufflepuff for a member's correct answer in class or just as impulsively deduct fifty points because some Ravenclaw students were boisterous in the halls. This obviously produces natural cohesion within each house.

But the cohesion between these particular friends, and especially Harry, Ron, and Hermione, is something more. There is

a normal amount of competition and badinage among them—
Hermione tends to preen herself as more of a scholar than the boys,
and Harry as captain of the Quidditch team has a certain amount
of dominance over Ron and Neville—but it is immediately obvious
that this group has a special bond and that Harry's fate will involve
the others as well. In the later volumes of the saga, when Harry is
acknowledged as the Chosen One—the one targeted for death and
at the same time slated to defeat Voldemort—there is no jealousy
among the others. They merely accept that he is their leader, and
even take lessons from him in overcoming the Dark Arts.

The Game of Life

Quidditch is one of Rowling's more interesting inventions,
and certainly an attraction for her sports-minded fans. Fasci-
natingly named—from the Latin *quid*, meaning "what," and much
bruited among the philosophers from Duns Scotus onward,
especially among the twentieth-century existentialists such as
Heidegger and Sartre, who delighted in discussing the "quiddity" of
things, their *what*ness or existence as objects—it is played with four
balls, three of which are menacingly alive and constantly attempt to
bludgeon the players. This is particularly dangerous because the
game is played on flying brooms.

As I write in *God, the Devil, and Harry Potter*, Quidditch is "a
game easily worthy of witches and wizards, involving lightning
speed, dexterity, teamwork, racing brooms, and not one but *four*
balls, three of which are aggressively *alive*, [and] it far surpasses
football, baseball, basketball, soccer, hockey, horse racing, and car
racing, all of whose actions it at least partially imitates, combines,
and sublimates."[24] Since writing that, I have realized that I should

have included jousting in the list of comparisons, for the players in Quidditch often appear to tilt at one another when trying to unseat an opponent.

Here I would like to quote my own description of the game, as I would find it difficult to improve on what I earlier said about it:

> Quidditch
> How to
> play —

There are <u>seven players</u> on each of two teams in a Quidditch match. <u>Three of the seven are called Chasers</u>, and they spend their time chasing a red ball about the size of a <u>soccer ball called the Quaffle</u> and trying to put it through one of six hoops mounted fifty feet in the air. (Harry describes the Chasers' actions as "sort of like basketball on broomsticks with six hoops.") One player on each team is a <u>Keeper.</u> It is the Keeper's job to fly around the hoops and prevent the other side from scoring. There are <u>two players on each team called Beaters.</u> The Beaters serve two functions: They rocket around the playing area trying to knock opposing players off their brooms, and they attempt to deflect the <u>Bludgers, the two lively black balls,</u> slightly smaller than the Quaffle, which zoom about dangerously toward the players during the contest. There is a seventh player on each team called the <u>Seeker.</u> This is a smaller, lighter player who buzzes about, often high above or around the periphery of the other action, looking for the <u>Golden Snitch, the small fourth ball, which has wings and darts about so quickly that it is difficult to see.</u> The game of Quidditch isn't ever over until the Snitch is caught by one of the Seekers, so games have been known to go on for months.

Harry Potter shows such amazing talent with a racing broom the first time he rides one that he is instantly marked for a Seeker.[25]

It is noteworthy that Rowling calls this team member a Seeker. The Seekers were a religious group that arose during the time of the Reformation and claimed to seek the kingdom of God in places other than human institutions because they believed the antichrist had corrupted all the formal church organizations. Today the term often indicates people who go from one religion or philosophy to another in search of a purer form of spirituality than they can usually find in any single place. Harry Potter is the best Seeker Hogwarts has ever seen.

The etymology of the word "snitch" is uncertain. It may derive from the Middle English *snachen*, which meant to give a sudden snap to something. (Our modern usage of "snitch" as a term for one who betrays another may be unrelated.) In the Quidditch games, the Golden Snitch snaps one way and then another without warning, and perhaps the art of catching it also has something to do with being able to snap it up, the way a baseball player snaps up a grounder. But beyond its name, the Golden Snitch is an important symbol, for securing it is the highest objective of the game of Quidditch. It is like the essence of life itself, which many people seek only to learn that it is highly elusive and difficult to capture. Quite aside from his claim to fame regarding Voldemort, Harry Potter, as the consummate Seeker, is qualified to be a leader among his fellow students and in the wizarding world in general. Everyone knows him because of his proficiency at catching the Snitch. To the families of the wizarding

Like the golden Ball in Fairy Tales.

world, he is like a popular football, basketball, baseball, or soccer star in the modern sports arena.

The Quidditch associations reinforce the idea of Harry as a Christ figure, because Christ was always in touch with the essence of life and encouraged others to be in touch with it for themselves. Even in the frequent duels between Jesus and leaders of the Pharisees and Sadducees, who frequently sought to entrap him in a question about the Torah, Jesus was invariably quicker than they were and leapt instinctively to the right answer to disarm them and capture an important truth for his audience. He was the greatest Seeker of all times, soaring where no one else has ever gone, and he understood more about "whatness" or "thisness" than anyone before or after him.

School Days, School Days…

In an episode of the old *Upstairs, Downstairs* BBC Masterpiece Theatre program, Lady Bellamy's small son is being taken off to school. A character comments that the British are the only people in the world who regularly commit their sons to the trying experience of being bundled off to boarding school while they are still in short pants and hanging on to their teddy bears. Such schools are the stuff of English fiction from Jane Austen and Charles Dickens to Evelyn Waugh, so J. K. Rowling easily obtained a sense of what they are like even if she didn't attend one herself. Life in such institutions is usually rigorous, masters are unreasonable, and children are at first lonely and disoriented. But being children, most of them are fairly resilient and manage to survive by aligning themselves with other children and an occasional professor.

Hogwarts is like no other school ever imagined. To begin with, the children travel north from London to get to the school, riding on the Hogwarts Express. Their train leaves from platform 9 3/4 in King's Cross Station, and at the beginning of every term it is packed with rollicking, expressive young wizards and witches headed to their magical destination. When they arrive, they are met by Hagrid, the huge, bearded man who is professor of the care of strange animals, and driven to the doors of a castle whose Great Hall boasts a refectory ceiling that imitates the condition of the sky; whose walls are filled with portrait subjects that talk to the students and move from frame to frame; and whose hallways are inhabited by ghosts who carry on as if they had the place all to themselves.

At the first meeting of the year, the Sorting Hat is brought out in the Great Hall—where thousands of candles float in the air and sparkling golden plates and goblets magically appear on the tables—and placed on each new child's head. The hat then announces the child's assigned house in a bold voice: Gryffindor, Hufflepuff, Ravenclaw, or Slytherin. Sometimes students cry because they don't get the house they want, and sometimes they rejoice at landing among friends or in a house to which their parents once belonged. But the hat is never wrong, and no one ever appeals its rulings.

Students take classes in a variety of esoteric subjects such as History of Magic, Herbology, Charms, Care of Magical Creatures, Magical Potions, Defense Against the Dark Arts, Divination, and Transfiguration. They learn charms, spells, potions, and curses that will enable them to survive in the world of wizardry. Some will become teachers themselves. Others will enter the Ministry of Magic, which has a huge bureaucracy in London, and still others will become merchants, restaurateurs, pub keepers, housewives, and more.

Outside the school is the Forbidden Forest, where one finds centaurs, serpents, enormous spiders, occasional giants, and the Whomping Willow—a huge old tree whose aggressive branches thrash its unfortunate victims within an inch of their lives. There is also Hogsmeade, the nearby wizarding town where students go on outings to visit the joke shop, pub, bookstore, and other places of interest.

Naturally, in an environment like this, students sometimes goof off, play pranks, and get into trouble, and Harry and his friends are no exception. With the Invisibility Cloak he inherited from his father, Harry—sometimes with his friends—sneaks around the school at forbidden hours. They party with the ghosts, look up strange old books in the library, and discover secret rooms and hidden passageways. Overall, though, they are good kids with sound values and a strong sense of loyalty to one another and to Dumbledore, and it is obvious that they will always choose to support good against evil.

Harry and his friends are acutely aware, even as they indulge in the hijinks characteristic of young teenagers, of the desperate battle between good and evil. Due to enchantment shields cast around Hogwarts, the children are mostly protected there, but they know that just outside they may encounter the dementors, the most hideous creatures in Lord Voldemort's service. Professor Lupin describes them to Harry Potter:

Dementors

Dementors are among the foulest creatures that walk this earth. They infest the darkest, filthiest places, they glory in decay and despair, they drain peace, hope, and happiness out of the air around them. Even Muggles feel their presence, though they can't see them. Get too near a dementor and every good feeling, every happy memory will be sucked out of you. If it can, the dementor will feed on you long enough to reduce you to something like itself…soul-less and evil. You'll be left with nothing but the worst experiences of your life.[26]

They must also worry about boggarts, creatures that shift their shapes to resemble the persons or situations individuals most fear. If one doesn't forget and become afraid of the boggarts, laughter and a spell called *Riddiculus* will dispel them. But it is often hard to recognize a boggart when one sees it because it seems so familiar and real.

Additionally, the students are keenly aware of Azkaban, the wizard equivalent of Alcatraz, where dementors freely suck the souls out of prisoners and leave them weak and powerless. George Weasley, Ron's brother, tells Harry about the time his father went on official business to Azkaban. "He said it was the worst place he'd ever been, he came back all weak and shaking…. They suck the happiness out of a place, dementors. Most of the prisoners go mad in there."[27] Harry's godfather, Sirius Black, is one of the few people to escape from Azkaban and live to tell about it. Harry and his friends know what an evil place it is and recognize how easily they might end up there if they fail against Voldemort and his supporters.

So, while they have fun like most youngsters off at boarding school, Harry and his friends appreciate the peril of their world and the ease with which it can destroy any of them. Their growing consciousness of Harry's role as the Chosen One, the Boy Who Lives, the one person capable of standing up to Voldemort, makes them prematurely circumspect, wise, and cautious. While the disciples of Jesus often seemed obtuse and insensitive to the dangers of their surroundings, so that Jesus called them blind, unhearing men who lacked faith and awareness, Harry's followers, like Harry himself, are almost invariably alert and ready to take on the evil in their world.

Instruction in Magic

A major part of discipleship involves learning: learning the master's ways, the master's craft, the master's teachings. Harry and his young followers are all students at Hogwarts, and it may seem questionable that a boy of Harry's tender years has something to teach to others.

Yet Rowling addresses this matter rather adroitly in volume five, *The Order of the Phoenix,* when Dolores Umbridge, who serves as professor of Defense Against the Dark Arts, is also promoted to Hogwarts High Inquisitor. Since Umbridge, working for the now corrupted ministry, has taught them little, Hermione insists that Harry become their instructor in Defense Against the Dark Arts so they can learn enough to pass their O.W.L.S., or Ordinary Wizarding Level exams, given at the end of their fifth year. Harry demurs, but Hermione mentions his victories over Voldemort to date and he eventually agrees. The group of about two dozen students meets in a secret place called the Room of Requirement. At first dubious of Harry's knowledge and ability to lead, the students eventually trust him and begin to cast effective defensive

Harry
instructs
in Magic.
group
Becomes
Dumbledor's
army

spells under his guidance.[28] They begin to call their little group Dumbledore's Army, indicating their perception of the coming of some kind of cataclysmic war.[29]

One of the major objections of some religious groups to the Potter stories is that they encourage youngsters to believe in witchcraft and magic. Perhaps the people in these groups overlook the amount of magic and wonderworking to which the Bible itself alludes, especially in the Gospels and the book of Acts. They would do well to read Professor Morton Smith's fascinating and well-documented book *Jesus the Magician: Charlatan or Son of God?*,[30] which examines the underlying theme of wizardry and superstition in the Roman world at the time of Jesus of Nazareth.

Smith notes three levels of magicians in the ancient world: the *goes* (plural *goeta*), or ordinary hack magician; the *magus, or wise man*, who had more finesse and was a level higher than the *goes*; and the *divine person,* the most exalted of the three, who was thought to be mystically connected with some divinity in order to manage the powers under his control. One reason the early church considered Jesus divine, says Smith, is simply that he possessed such uncanny awareness and performed so many wonders of healing and physical restoration. The Gospel of Matthew records, for example, how "great crowds came to him, bringing with them the lame, the maimed, the blind, the mute, and many others. They put them at his feet, and he cured them, so that the crowd was amazed when they saw the mute speaking, the maimed whole, the lame walking, and the blind seeing. And they praised the God of Israel" (Matt 15:30–31).

Perhaps the most gratuitous miracle attributed to Jesus is the one recorded in Mark 11:12–14, 20–24, about the cursing of the fig tree. As Jesus and the disciples walked from Bethany to Jerusalem, they passed a fig tree in leaf. Jesus, being hungry, went to find some figs, but there were none. "May no one ever eat fruit from you again," he said. Passing the tree the next morning, they saw that the tree had "withered away to its roots." Peter said, "Rabbi, look! The fig tree that you cursed has withered." Jesus responded, "Have faith in God. Truly I tell you, if you say to this mountain, 'Be taken up and thrown into the sea,' and if you do not doubt in your heart, but believe that what you say will come to pass, it will be done for you." This is the only miracle recorded in the New Testament in which Jesus casts a spell on any living thing, and the only one involving an inanimate object.

Communion

Smith's *Jesus the Magician* offers a fascinating discussion of the Eucharist, or eating of the god, as the most secret and magical of all of Jesus' gifts. The Eucharist was not an uncommon occurrence in the ancient world—the Greek mystery religions often featured a meal in which the divinity was consumed—and was supposed to have the greatest power to unite the partakers with their god. We have become so accustomed to eating the Eucharist that we easily overlook what a magical event it was for early Christians. St. Paul even warned the Christians in Corinth, who were behaving poorly when they assembled to receive the Lord's Supper, that eating and drinking unworthily brought judgment upon them and caused many of them to become weak or ill, and some even to die! (1 Cor 11:27–32)

Thus, Rowling isn't far off the mark when she uses witchcraft and magic in the Harry Potter novels: if she was writing a basically Christian saga or an overlay of the Christian story with a story about a boy wizard—which I believe she was—then wonder-

working has an integral role in her narrative. In addition to all the
miracles in the Gospels, think about some of the stories in the book
of Acts: Jesus ascends into heaven before the disciples' eyes (1:9);
the people gathered at the Feast of Pentecost receive the gift of
understanding other languages, and tongues of fire dance on their
foreheads (2:1–4); Peter and John heal a man lame from birth
(3:1–10); a couple named Ananias and Sapphira are struck dead for
lying about their possessions (5:1–11); people are healed of
lameness and illness when Peter's shadow falls on them (5:14–16);
Saul is struck with temporary blindness on the road to Damascus,
then receives his sight again when a man named Ananias visits him
(9:1–19); Peter heals a man who has been a paralytic for eight years
(9:32–33). All of these wonders occur within the first *third* of the
book of Acts! Clearly, Rowling has only extended the sense of
magic and the supernatural from the first years of the church into
the present time and employed it to embellish her story about a boy
wizard and the world as he viewed it.

A Growing Awareness

As mentioned, Harry encounters Voldemort as an infant and
receives from the Dark Lord a lightning-shaped scar that aches
whenever Voldemort is either near or planning a particularly
vicious attack. Harry's first ten years, spent in the unpleasant
household of the Dursleys where he is treated with disdain by his
Aunt Petunia and Uncle Vernon and cousin Dudley, are the safest
years of his life. Dumbledore later tells him he placed Harry with
his relatives because the boy needed to be safe while he was growing
up. From the moment Harry leaves number 4 Privet Drive to go to
Hogwarts, it is a different story: he repeatedly encounters

Voldemort and his minions despite the relative protection of the school.

During this period of growing self-awareness and understanding of his "calling," two things are significant for Harry's friends if they are to develop in ways that parallel Jesus' disciples: (1) a growing awareness on their part of who Harry is and what his mission entails, and (2) a commensurate loyalty to him and his mission. All three members of his inner circle of friends earn top scores on both counts.

Like Jesus, Harry experiences an increasing amount of talk about him everywhere, not only among his followers; thus, part of his followers' growing realization of his special nature is a natural consequence of his mounting public notoriety. Rita Skeeter, the sensationalist reporter who frequently snoops around Hogwarts and the Ministry of Magic searching for a story, is responsible for some of Harry's fame. Her articles about him fuel rumors in the wizarding world. However, much of the talk arises more or less spontaneously out of the strong expectations that have swirled around Harry since his famous encounter with Voldemort as a baby. He is the messianic hope of all who seek liberation from Voldemort's destructive sway, and every time he has another noteworthy encounter with the Dark Lord, rumors spread once more like dry leaves in a strong wind.

While every book details Harry's encounters with Voldemort or his representatives, their ferocity grows noticeably in volume five, *The Order of the Phoenix*, in which the officials at the Ministry of Magic turn against Dumbledore and Harry—completing what begins at the end of book four, *The Goblet of Fire*. In book five, they declare that Lord Voldemort did not actually return and dismiss the increasing power of the Dark Lord's friends, a typical government pronouncement in the face of a monstrous crisis. Special Assistant to the Minister of Magic Dolores Umbridge sends dementors to attack Harry and his cousin Dudley Dursley (who after a flabby childhood has surprisingly metamorphosed into a heavyweight boxing champion), and she and her friends in the ministry wage a campaign in *The Daily Prophet* to discredit Harry's report that he met and fought with Voldemort. Then, as if to cap Umbridge's ascendancy in officialdom, she is sent to Hogwarts to "teach" Defense Against the Dark Arts, effectively stifling students' learning in this vital area, terrorizing the children, and making life miserable for the kinder, gentler faculty members.

After illegally using magic to repel the dementors sent by Umbridge, Harry stands trial at the Ministry of Magic. Dumbledore produces a surprise witness who confirms Harry's story, and ultimately the boy is cleared of all charges and allowed to return to school.

At school, Harry dreams of a room at the Ministry of Magic that supposedly contains a secret weapon Voldemort desires. Rowling later reveals that Voldemort is invading Harry's mind to implant these visions in a process called Legilimency. When Harry tells Ron and Hermione about a particular vision in which he sees his beloved godfather, Sirius Black, in danger at the ministry, Hermione responds, "You...This isn't a criticism, Harry! But you do...sort of...I mean—don't you think you've got a bit of a—a—*saving-people-thing*?" [31] It resembles the objections Jesus' disciples sometimes gave as they argued with him at times about the legitimacy of his calling or his need to stand against the scribes and Pharisees who took over the religion of Israel. Voldemort's efforts eventually draw Harry and his friends—including Neville Longbottom, Ron's sister Ginny, and Luna Lovegood, who were loving followers of the sort associated with Jesus—to the Ministry of Magic to try to rescue Sirius.

After searching through various mysterious rooms, the children find the room Harry saw in his dream; they see rows of shelves filled with glass balls containing prophecies. Voldemort wants the one that reveals his connection to Harry, and only Harry can get it. The moment Ron finds the right prophecy and hands it to Harry, black shapes materialize in the air around them—Death Eaters, Voldemort's followers, with wands pointed directly at the children's hearts.

Now Harry learns the dream was Voldemort's way to get the prophecy, and he and his friends quickly use magic to cause a distraction that results in the shelves crashing around them. As hundreds of prophecy balls shatter, the children run for their lives. They end up battling the Death Eaters, helped by the arrival of members of the Order of the Phoenix, powerful wizards fighting for Dumbledore's cause. Like Jesus' disciples, the children experience difficulty and even harm as they try to defend what they believe. In this book, for the first time, Harry's friends have a clear awareness of why they follow him. The answer lies in the prophecy itself: "The one with the power to vanquish the dark lord approaches…and the dark lord will mark him as his equal, but he will have power the dark lord knows not…and either must die at the hand of the other for neither can live while the other survives."[32]

In future volumes—*The Half-Blood Prince* and *The Deathly Hallows*—there is no question about why these friends are loyal to

Harry and his mission. The Ministry of Magic publicizes false reports about the incident in the Hall of Prophecy—blaming the attempted theft on dementors—but news about Harry's being "the Chosen One" spreads everywhere, and his friends realize with certainty, if they had doubted before, that he is the one fated to oppose the evil Lord Voldemort. Despite the danger involved, they volunteer to accompany Harry in his search for the remaining four Horcruxes in which Voldemort has secreted parts of his spirit so Harry can destroy them.

In *Half-Blood Prince*, Ron assures Harry, "We're with you whatever happens"[33]; his words are eerily reminiscent of a promise Simon Peter made to Jesus: "Lord, I am ready to go with you to prison and to death!" (Luke 22:33). As in the case of Peter, who would deny his Lord, Ron later quarrels with Harry and defects for a period of time. After suffering a terrible injury by Voldemort's followers, Ron's fear of the Dark Lord intensifies. While the three hide away in the forest in *Deathly Hallows*, trying to discern their next step in locating the Horcruxes, Ron demands that they return to the old habit of calling Voldemort "You-Know-Who." Harry says Dumbledore told them not to be afraid of a name, but Ron reminds them that Dumbledore is dead: "In case you hadn't noticed, mate...calling You-Know-Who by his name didn't do Dumbledore much good in the end. Just—just show You-Know-Who some respect, will you?"[34]

Increasingly, Harry's scar troubles him: he knows Voldemort is planning something. Stress and isolation heighten the tension, resulting in arguments, unfounded suspicions about each other, and desperate fears for loved ones. Finally, the boys draw their wands on one another, and only Hermione's intervention stops

Ron defects from Harry.

them from going farther. Just as Peter tersely denied Christ, Ron turns away from Harry then, striding out into the rain. He is gone for weeks.

Harry and silver white doe Patronus

Sometime later, Harry walks through the dark forest and sees a silver light ahead of him. It comes from a Patronus, a protective spell whose appearance differs from person to person, and is in the shape of a silver-white doe. The Patronus leads Harry deeper into the forest to a small, frozen pool, and then it disappears. He realizes

Sword of Gryffindor at bottom of pool.
Cold baptism

that the sword of Gryffindor lies at the bottom of the pool. After breaking the icy surface with a spell, Harry jumps into the pool to retrieve the sword—a kind of cold baptism. Suddenly, the chain around his neck, which holds a Horcrux in the form of a locket, tightens and begins to choke him. He feels himself drowning, but then someone pulls him from the water. Harry regains

Chokes on Horcrux locket.

consciousness beside the pool and finds that Ron has returned and now holds the sword in one hand and the locket in the other. "How come you're here?" Harry asks. Ron stutters, "Well, I've—you know—I've come back. If…You know. You still want me."[35] It

Ron comes back – Saves Harry.

is like Simon Peter's return to Jesus after his defection. Later, Ron remembers that Dumbledore was the last person to have the sword of Gryffindor and wonders if the doe Patronus represented their former headmaster. Ron assumes Dumbledore "must have known I'd run out on you." "No," Harry insists. "He must've known

Last battle.

you'd always want to come back."[36]

However, near the end of the story, in the epic battle at Hogwarts between Dumbledore's Army and the forces of Voldemort, Harry's supporters never waver. Ron, Hermione, and Neville fight bravely against overwhelming odds. When Ron and Hermione think Harry is dead, their grief is immediate and intense.[37] Neville Longbottom actually charges at Voldemort in anger, though Voldemort easily disarms him and throws him to the ground. When the Dark Lord learns that Neville comes from a distinctive family of purebloods, he showers the boy with praise and invites him to become one of his Death Eaters. Neville refuses, shouting, "Dumbledore's Army!"[38]

In the last moments of battle, Voldemort summons the Sorting Hat from the school, intending to destroy it since he claims all students will henceforth be Slytherins. He forces the hat onto Neville's head, flicks his wand, and watches as the hat and Neville ignite. At this instant, Harry decides to act, and hundreds of members of Dumbledore's Army swarm over the walls toward the castle.

Neville moves swiftly, and the flaming hat falls off his head. From its depths comes something silver with a ruby-studded handle—the sword of Gryffindor! Seizing the sword's handle, Neville swings it in a mighty arc and severs the head of Voldemort's great snake Nagini while a phalanx of centaurs charges, scattering the crowd of Death Eaters. Harry duels with Voldemort, and Voldemort—Tom Riddle—slumps to the floor in death.

The battle is over, and Harry's friends have proven faithful and true. Like the disciples of Jesus, they are momentarily routed. But in the end they are strong and loyal. Years later, as described in the epilogue, they remain close friends.

3

VOLDEMORT AND THE NATURE OF EVIL

The nature of evil has been a topic of philosophical discourse from time immemorial. Plato thought it had to do with the difference between our perception of the real world and the truly real world of an ideal plane or the realm of intellectual forms. When people understand the ideal world and aspire to it, there is less distortion or evil in the world they actually inhabit. Augustine, who knew Platonic doctrine, argued that God made the world good and human beings distort it by their sinful rebellion against him. Thomas Aquinas reasoned that, as God is perfect, angels are almost perfect, and human beings and other creatures on the hierarchy of substances cannot attain to the higher order of perfection. Instead, they exist in a state of sinfulness and imperfection, living only by God's grace. Reformation theologian John Calvin carried Thomism to an extreme by declaring that all flesh is born in sin, and even little babies will go to hell unless providentially spared. The rationalist philosophers of the seventeenth and eighteenth centuries reacted to such extremism by drawing up logical views of the world that essentially attributed all sin and evil to an imperfect understanding of the way things work, and initiated the secularist rebellion against religion that eventually resulted in modern atheism. The existentialists of the twentieth century, reacting against both religion and rationalism, sought to understand evil or its secular equivalent as a failure of the self to value itself in a world of things and other selves, and made virtues of self-recognition and self-control. The dialogue about sin and evil, in other words, is an ongoing discourse that isn't likely to end as long as even two human beings remain on the planet.

Of course, evil in the abstract and evil in personal experience are totally different. It is one thing to recognize evil in the megalomania of Adolph Hitler and it is another thing to be a Jew who experienced a concentration camp firsthand or whose relatives suffered in one.

As I began this chapter, I was interrupted by a phone call from a friend several states away who reported that her husband was in jail. When I expressed my dismay, she told me the story. On numerous medications for various problems, yesterday afternoon her husband began drinking with a friend. He came home while she was still at work and became verbally and physically abusive to her two teenage daughters from a previous marriage. In an altercation with one of them, he pulled out a fistful of her hair, and she bit him so badly that he bled. One of the girls called the police, who came and took the man to jail.

My friend's husband is normally a sweet, mild-mannered man who laughs easily, has a self-deprecating sense of humor, and is friendly and entertaining. His actions seemed totally out of character to me. Yet I have known enough alcoholics and drug abusers to realize that my friend's story wasn't as preposterous as it sounded. Her husband was the victim of his own weaknesses. After a moderately successful life, he became less successful and was reduced to working away from home for extended periods. He dreamed of a better life for himself and his family, but the dreams were slow in reaching fulfillment. Alcohol made him feel better temporarily. When he and the girls began to fight, he was victimized by his own sense of personal failure and took it out on them. A psychologist once told him that he tended to fall into a rage because he felt depressed. It was a sad story.

J. K. Rowling, in positing a world divided against itself, bravely took on the task of explaining evil in that world. Why are some people content to live in ordinary ways, and why are others unhappy unless they can control the happy people and make them live as they insist? Why does Tom Riddle become the evil Lord Voldemort and Harry Potter become the hero who defeats him? Rowling doesn't pretend to be a philosopher or a theologian; she is only a fabulist, a storyteller. But she has told the story of all humanity—its foibles and errors, its witting and unwitting sins, its inability to get along peacefully and harmoniously without fighting and wars and hatred.

The Riddle of Tom Riddle

How does a smart, talented young man like Tom Marvolo Riddle—a.k.a. Lord Voldemort—become so twisted and malevolent? What factors in his background account for his behavior? Or is it merely something innate in him—perhaps in his DNA—that makes him who he is? The enigma is probably insoluble, but Rowling gives us much to think about.

Through the first three books in Rowling's series, we encounter only the wicked side of Lord Voldemort and the derivative vileness of his followers. We find him in the surly Draco Malfoy, whose father, Lucius, influences the Ministry of Magic and is also a Death Eater, and in Draco's blustering, posturing friends Crabbe and Goyle. We suspect his influence on Severus Snape, the sinister Hogwarts professor whose life Harry's father once saved but who now sneers at Harry and his friends, and we see him openly in Professor Quirrell, the two-faced wizard who tries to kill Harry and his friends in *The Sorcerer's Stone.* Voldemort is somehow linked to the deadly basilisk in *The Chamber of Secrets* and the hundreds of dementors who attack Harry in *The Prisoner of Azkaban.* We hear from Firenze, the noble centaur, that Voldemort is responsible for the deaths of unicorns in the forest. To this point, we are more aware of Voldemort as a menace than as a real, existing individual.

But the suspense builds. In volume three, *The Prisoner of Azkaban*, Professor Sibyll Trelawney, who teaches Divination at Hogwarts, goes into a trance and predicts in a strange voice, "The Dark Lord lies alone and friendless, abandoned by his followers. His servant has been chained these twelve years. Tonight, before midnight...the servant will break free and set out to rejoin his master. The Dark Lord will rise again with his servant's aid, greater and more terrible than ever he was. Tonight...before midnight...the servant...will set out...to rejoin...his master...."[39]

The chained servant Trelawney mentions is Peter Pettigrew, whom Harry's godfather Sirius Black unsuccessfully attempted to kill twelve years earlier. Like Sirius, Peter is an Animagus, a person who can transform into an animal; in Peter's case the animal, appropriately, is a rat. For years, he masquerades as Ron Weasley's pet rat Scabbers, getting an inside track on the Ministry of Magic through Ron's father, Arthur Weasley, who works there, and observing Harry and Ron's other friends and teachers at Hogwarts.

Remus Lupin, Harry's professor for one year and also a werewolf, tells Harry about his own group of friends when he was a student at Hogwarts—Harry's father James, Sirius Black, and Peter Pettigrew. As a token of their friendship to Lupin, these three learned to become Animagi in order to turn into animals at will and keep him company. James became Prongs, a magnificent stag; Sirius became Padfoot, a huge black dog; and Peter became Wormtail, a rat. Using James's Invisibility Cloak, they sneaked out of Hogwarts every month when the moon was full and Lupin transformed into a werewolf, changing themselves into animals to accompany him. While on these forays, they discovered all the secret paths, passages, tunnels, and hiding places that they drew onto a Marauder's Map Harry receives from Fred and George Weasley. Sirius Black reveals that Pettigrew told Voldemort where to find James and Lily Potter the night he killed them and scarred their son. Now Pettigrew is back at Hogwarts because the Dark Lord is regaining strength and needs information about Harry and his friends.

Rowling begins volume four, *The Goblet of Fire,* with a scene in a creepy old house in Little Hangleton called "the Riddle House." Pettigrew, or Wormtail, is present with the weak, secretive figure of Voldemort that speaks in a cold, hissing voice about revenge on Harry Potter. A giant snake named Nagini also slithers around the room. A short time later, panic overtakes those attending the Quidditch World Cup match, hidden deep in the woods away from the Muggles, when a giant skull fills the night sky over the campers, flashing with thousands of emerald stars as a serpent protrudes from its mouth like a waving tongue. "It's the Dark Mark, Harry!" exclaims Hermione. "You-Know-Who's sign!"[40] People begin screaming and running in all directions. Suddenly, twenty wizards appear around Harry, Hermione, and Ron, their wands pointed at the three young people. Harry's wand was indeed used to conjure the Dark Mark—but not by him. A house-elf named Winky has it, but claims that she picked it up off the ground where she found it. Meanwhile, some wizards round up the Death Eaters they can locate and check their memories. Three days earlier, Harry's scar had burned. Now this. What does it portend?

Later in the same novel, Harry actually beholds Voldemort for the first time since his infancy. Engaged in the Triwizard Tournament, Harry pauses at the end of a difficult race to allow his chief competitor from Hufflepuff House, a boy named Cedric Diggory, to share the glory of winning with him. Suddenly, as they both hold the winner's cup, they are transported to a remote graveyard hundreds of miles from the site of the races: the winner's cup has been turned into a Portkey that brings them to this deserted place where they behold Wormtail carrying a bundle.

Harry's scar explodes with pain as he hears a cold voice say, "Kill the spare." A blast of green light blazes through his eyelids, and Cedric falls down dead from the *Avada Kedavra* killing curse.

As Nagini slithers nearby, Wormtail binds Harry and conjures a large cauldron atop crackling flames. "It is ready, master," he says. Then Wormtail opens his robes, revealing a hideous sight. The bundle he carries has "the shape of a crouched human child, except that Harry had never seen anything less like a child. It was hairless and scaly-looking, a dark, raw, reddish black. Its arms and legs were

[margin note: Encounter with Voldemort]

thin and feeble, and its face—no child alive ever had a face like that—flat and snakelike, with gleaming red eyes."[41]

Wormtail drops the creature into the cauldron and pronounces an incantation. Then he completes an elaborate ritual including cutting off his own hand and slicing into Harry's arm to collect the boy's blood, narrating his actions as he drops the items into the cauldron. Harry prays that the creature has drowned. Instead, a pale figure rises in the steam from the water.

Voldemort rises from the cauldron.

"Robe me," commands the cold voice. Wormtail does. "The thin man stepped out of the cauldron, staring at Harry…and Harry stared back into the face that had haunted his nightmares for three years. Whiter than a skull, with wide, livid scarlet eyes and a nose that was flat as a snake's with slits for nostrils…Lord Voldemort had risen again."[42]

Voldemort tells Harry that the boy is lying on the grave of Voldemort's own father, a Muggle whom he killed years before for deserting his witch mother—a man named Tom Riddle, who gave his name to the young Voldemort. "But look, Harry!" says Voldemort. "My *true* family returns.…"[43] Death Eaters appear among all the tombstones—among them Lucius Malfoy and the senior Crabbe and Goyle—falling to their knees and kissing the hem of Voldemort's robe. Voldemort reviews his troops and commends them for their work. Then he turns back to Harry, explaining to the Death Eaters that he has been unable to touch the boy for years due to the mantle of protection cast over him by his mother's sacrifice. Until this night, he has been powerless since his encounter with the child, which left him without a body and with the lone power of possessing the bodies of others.

Voldemort killed his father.

Voldemort uses Harrys blood to revive.

But now, using Harry's blood—and thanks to Wormtail's devotion—his body has returned, and he is ready for vengeance. He torments Harry with the *Cruciatus* curse, causing the boy pain "beyond anything he had ever experienced; his very bones were on fire; his head was surely splitting along his scar; his eyes were rolling madly in his head; he wanted it to end... to black out... to die...." Voldemort insists that he will kill Harry Potter here and now, "with no Dumbledore to help him, and no mother to die for him."[44]

First encounter with Voldemort since death.

However, Voldemort allows Harry to defend himself with a wand. The older, stronger evil wizard seems to have the upper hand, continuing to torture Harry as the Death Eaters look on and laugh. Finally, Harry uses his Quidditch skills to roll behind a tombstone and avoid a spell. He stands and shouts, "*Expelliarmus!*" at Voldemort, just as Voldemort shouts, "*Avada Kedavra!*" at him. The thread of golden light from their two wands meets, merges, and lifts them both into the air. Then the thread splinters, forming a golden, dome-shaped web around them, keeping the Death Eaters away.

Harry hears the music of a phoenix song. It buoys Harry's spirit—the Holy Spirit bearing up his spirit!—and, with the help of departed loved ones, he holds his ground with Voldemort. Finally, he is able to dart back to Cedric's side, grasp his wrist with one hand and the Portkey with the other, and transport them back to Hogwarts.

This powerful scene from *Goblet of Fire* is Harry's first face-to-face encounter with Voldemort since he was a baby, but it will not be his last. Harry meets Voldemort in various ways in each succeeding volume, learning more and more about his mortal enemy.

He learns that Voldemort, as Tom Riddle, was a student at Hogwarts; that he forsook his Muggle ancestry and devoted himself to the purity of the wizarding line; that he worked hard to master the Dark Arts; that he once insisted that Dumbledore let him teach Defense Against the Dark Arts; that he learned the darkest art of all, how to implant parts of himself in Horcruxes as protection against death; and that of the three Deathly Hallows—the Elder Wand, the Resurrection Stone, and the Invisibility Cloak—he sought the first, thinking it would give him the most power.

At the graveyard, Harry listens as Voldemort reminds his Death Eaters, "You know my goal—to conquer death."[45] For the time being, it appears that he has done it.

The Little People Who Permit Evil to Hold Sway

Who are Voldemort's followers, the Death Eaters? They are ordinary witches and wizards, for the most part: people like Pettigrew, or Wormtail, who ally themselves to him out of fear or out of the desire to share in his extraordinary power; people who wouldn't be considered evil under normal circumstances, but who, when aligned with Voldemort, become tainted by evil. They are seldom powerful in their own right. Most of them are lackeys, underlings who dream of being somebody and are willing to sell their souls for a mess of pottage or an ounce of recognition.

Bellatrix Lestrange, first mentioned in *The Goblet of Fire* and revealed more clearly in the last two volumes of the septet, is more powerful than most. Many of Voldemort's followers are like Lucius Malfoy, however, functionaries in the Ministry of Magic whose presence there keeps Voldemort informed and undermines the good that others in the ministry try to accomplish. Theirs is a derivative evil—evil by association—more than something springing from the depths of their own wicked beings. They lie, cheat, and dissemble on behalf of the Dark Lord, not on their own account, and thus exist largely as adumbrations of his dark soul.

Increasingly, as we read through the seven volumes of the saga, we witness the Ministry of Magic's gradual subversion to the shadowy power and machinations of evil. Those in power begin to suborn basically good people. We see this habit all too often in our own government: young people swayed by titles, offices, and promotions who eventually believe that what they do is not only significant but right. Twenty years later, they inhabit the same halls and offices, but with better views and bigger perks, and congratulate themselves on making it so far. They spend their odd hours dreaming of retirement and using their bonuses and 401(k)s. More often than not, they have lent minimal power and agreement to the plans and policies of their superiors without questioning ethics or morality, and have washed down any pangs of guilt with a shot of tequila or a cocktail paid for by their generous expense accounts. Without intending to, they become complicit in the sins of omission and commission by their group or party in power and will go to their graves defending their records as upstanding, reliable citizens.

In her book *Plan B*, Anne Lamott tells the piquant story of A. J. Maste, a man who for years stood outside the White House with a candle every night, whatever the weather, to protest the U.S. government's war in Vietnam. One night a reporter spotted him there, sheltering his candle from the rain in lonely vigil. He asked,

"Do you really think what you are doing will change the country?" *I do this*
"Oh no," Maste responded. "I do not expect to change the country, *so the*
I do this so that the country will not change me." [46] Unfortunately, *will not*
some people do not have as much integrity and awareness as Maste *change me.*
did.

Even Percy Weasley, Ron's older brother, becomes overly
ambitious to get ahead in the Ministry of Magic, to rise to some
larger position of power and responsibility. Though the earlier
books in the series portray him as an intelligent leader of his
Hogwarts peers, he grows ashamed of his father's place in the
ministry; rather than striving to rise to the top, Arthur Weasley
remains a faithful and lowly servant in the Misuse of Muggle
Artifacts department. Eventually, Percy wants nothing to do with
his father, with Harry, or with his younger brothers, Ron, George,
and Fred. When Percy eventually tries to make amends in *The
Deathly Hallows*, Fred says he has been a "Ministry-loving, family-
disowning, power-hungry moron." [47]

In contrast, when Rufus Scrimgeour is Minister of Magic and
attempts to recruit Harry so the ministry can exploit his popularity
for its own ends, Harry refuses, saying he doesn't "want to be
used." [48]

The Importance of Jokes

The nature of evil is anything but funny, but those fighting
for the other side sometimes survive on humor alone. Thus, the
jokes in Rowling's series are essential as a counterpoint to the
boredom and complications of bureaucracy. Bureaucracy is almost
invariably bland and aimless, incapable at its best of becoming
more than a mere minding of p's and q's, and likely at its worst to

yield to abuse and mismanagement. Jokes, on the other hand, require creativity. They spring out of sudden wit and insight. They declare that there is more to life than this, that there is dash and fun and creativity.

In *The Anatomy of an Illness*, Norman Cousins writes about the death sentence he received from his doctors. He says he struggled out of his hospital bed to get to a hotel room by himself, where he watched a constant stream of videos of old comedic films—Buster Keaton, the Three Stooges, Laurel and Hardy—and laughed himself back to health and wholeness. Man does not live by tragedy alone. Levity offers mysterious depths of healing.

In *The Goblet of Fire*, after giving the gold from his Triwizard winnings to Fred and George Weasley to help fund their new joke shop, Harry tells them, "Listen, if you don't take it, I'm throwing it down the drain. I don't want it and I don't need it. But I could do with a few laughs. We could all do with a few laughs. I've got a feeling we're going to need them more than usual before long."[49]

Rowling is at her inventive best when fashioning the practical jokes the Weasley brothers market—Ton-Tongue Toffee, which lengthens the victim's tongue to four or five feet; fake wands that turn into giant rubber mice and other things; Weasleys' Wildfire Whiz-bangs, with giant pink Catherine wheels that fly through the air and sparklers that write swear words of their own accord—and other funny, imaginative touches such as living portraits, enchanted basement windows that mimic ordinary windows looking out on the world, knives that chop vegetables all by themselves, and wastepaper baskets that swallow trash and then belch. These rib-ticklers abound in Rowling's books and serve to make the grim stories of dementors, Death Eaters, and deadly conflict more bearable. Clearly, humor of this sort has served Rowling personally through her years of hardship and penury, and she sees it as an antidote to life's smaller and larger tragedies.

Byron wrote in *Don Juan*, "And if I laugh at any mortal thing, / 'Tis that I may not weep." Certainly humor is a valid way of facing the less pleasant aspects of human existence. According to Elton Trueblood's *The Humor of Christ*, Jesus frequently employed humor—for example, he said it is easier for a camel to pass through the eye of a needle than for a rich man to enter into heaven (Mark 10:25)—to teach important lessons or counter his enemies.[50]

The End of Evil?

In Rowling's view, evil in the world ebbs and flows, declines and flourishes, much as bad weather, plagues, and the economy do. We can only assume that, were Rowling to write another septet of volumes, the cycle of evil and oppression would start up again for a second series of engaging tales in which good and evil are pitted against one another as before. The centaur Firenze, who serves for a time as Divination teacher at Hogwarts, sees everything from an extra-human viewpoint and sagely comments on this periodicity: "the indications have been that Wizard-kind is living through nothing more than a brief calm between two wars. Mars, bringer of battle, shines brightly above us, suggesting that the fight must break out again soon."[51]

Christianity's way of dealing with the ongoing problem of evil, and the one Rowling adopts, is summarized in Jesus' parable of the wheat and the tares: good and evil must grow together until the end of everything and the final judgment that follows it. This explanation seems as good as any; regardless, it is the one Rowling adopts. If in the end her handling of the problem seems indeterminate and lacking in finality, it is because she appears to accept the Christian mythology she follows—that Christ's death and resurrection dealt evil a mortal blow, but evil must continue to exact its toll on human nature until the end of time, when the heavenly scenario envisioned by the writer of the Apocalypse (Revelation) will take place and all human beings, dead and alive, will be judged for their faithfulness to God and the Son of God.

There is peace—and apparently happiness—in the wizarding world after the death of Voldemort. But, as the world does not end at that time, is it a final peace? Answering this question is not Rowling's intention, as she only mimics the Christian story. Eventually, followers of Christ had to cope with the fact that Jesus did not return to earth as immediately as they anticipated; therefore, they adjusted their views to accommodate an ongoing world that looked pretty much the way it had always looked. Christians will tell you that the world is different since Christ—that they handle the problem of evil differently than humans did before Jesus—but to others it appears much as it always has, characterized by frequent spasms of improvement and deterioration.

One cannot help wondering, for example, about Draco Malfoy, whom Harry, Ron, Hermione, and Ginny see on platform 9 3/4 at King's Cross Station nineteen years after Harry vanquishes the Dark Lord. Like them, Draco is sending his child on the express train to Hogwarts. In the end, Draco proves less villainous and hopeless than he appears through most of the volumes of the Potter story. He cannot bring himself to kill Dumbledore as Voldemort commissions him to do in *The Half-Blood Prince*, and *The Deathly Hallows* explains that much of his apparent loyalty to the Dark One owes more to fear for his father in Azkaban than any genuine attachment he might have to evil. Yet he is still not entirely comfortable with Harry and his friends. At the station, "Draco caught sight of Harry, Ron, Hermione, and Ginny staring at him, nodded curtly, and turned away again."[52] We learn that Draco named his son Scorpius—a name as indicative of venom and untrustworthiness as Draco's own.

What, if anything, is Rowling saying through this vignette in the epilogue of her lengthy narrative? That history will repeat itself? That people never forget, even years after graduation from school and eventful pilgrimages through life, the hurts and enmities of former times, so that even on the best occasions there remains a shadow of regret or pain over their lives? We cannot be certain, of course; perhaps Rowling herself couldn't tell us. She was merely tying up loose ends, tucking them in like a craftsperson finishing a basket, so that they didn't dangle unappetizingly from the sides or the bottom. Or maybe she was reminding us, ever so faintly, of the way things can start up again after a period of quiescence.

Samuel Beckett does this in *Waiting for Godot*: every time we think the action is essentially over, that Godot has either come or is not coming, there is some small hint to the contrary. It is a delicate balancing act, a nuanced performance intended to say as much by the inconclusiveness itself as by anything overtly stated.

It is basically an ending that does not end, which brings us back to the conclusion that Rowling is indeed mimicking the Christian story. It too has a certain cyclical quality, even while purporting to be linear and straightforward. Christ has come but is still coming. Christendom has its ups and downs, its ebb and flow;

there are periods of lethargy and periods of revival. Things wind down, and then they wind up again. Expectancy wanes, then flourishes.

4

HARRY POTTER AS SACRIFICIAL LAMB

In most great passion narratives—certainly in *Billy Budd, The Idiot,* and *The Greek Passion*—the Christ figures are hapless victims, innocent men who happen to fall askew of the world around them and are crucified for it. Not so with Rowling's Harry Potter. Harry, owing to his unhappy childhood in the Dursley household and his frequent encounters with evil after he becomes a student at Hogwarts, is one of the most preternaturally wary young men in all literature. Like an urchin in a Dickens novel, he has learned by the tender age of twelve or thirteen to lie, dissemble, and keep secrets, if only in order to survive.

This is one of the reasons religious conservatives dislike Harry and urge parents not to let their children read the Potter stories. Like most Pharisees, they cleanse the outside of the cup and leave the inside untouched, or strain at gnats and end by swallowing camels. I believe they also forget what it is like to be a child and fend for oneself in a complex world of competing loyalties, baffling hormonal development, and sometimes faithless friends. Lying— especially of the "white lie" variety—happens to them as naturally as breathing, for it is a coping mechanism for dealing with difficult situations. As for breaking rules or disobeying orders from time to time—well, the *unco guid* should remember that Jesus himself was never strict about obeying the rules and constantly angered the scribes and Pharisees with his stubbornly rebellious spirit.

After all, the idea of Jesus' sinlessness is a silly notion offered by some theologians in the early church who derived the idea from their earlier conclusion that he was a sacrificial lamb—"Behold, the Lamb of God," John the Baptist says of Jesus in the Fourth Gospel, the most literarily contrived of all the Gospels—and therefore, like the birds and animals sold in the temple for propitiatory sacrifices, was supposedly "without spot or blemish." Once seized upon, the idea became stitched into the church's sacrificial theology. Jesus was the pure and spotless Son of the Father. As the author of Hebrews says, alternating between the images of Christ as priest and Christ as sacrifice—talk about having it both ways!—"We do not have a high priest who is unable to sympathize with our weaknesses, but we have one who in every respect has been tested as we are, *yet without sin*" (Heb 4:15, my italics). Later, commending the image of Christ as sacrifice, the same author writes of the blood of goats and calves and then speaks of the much higher worth of Christ's blood, "who through the eternal Spirit offered himself *without blemish* to God" (Heb 9:14, my italics). The Apostle Peter expresses the same understanding, arguing that we were ransomed "not with perishable things like silver or gold, but with the precious blood of Christ, like that of a lamb *without defect or blemish*" (1 Pet 1:18-19, my italics).

In turn, early Christian writers employed the idea of spotlessness to encourage a similar immaculateness on the part of believers themselves, as in this reference in 2 Peter: "Therefore, beloved,

[margin note: ? Jesus as sinless is a silly notion.]

while you are waiting for these things, strive to be found by him at peace, *without spot or blemish*" (3:14, my italics). Commendable as this description may have been, however, some Christians today regard it as an unnecessary corollary to doctrine and an embellishment whose significance has ceased to signify anything of value. What does it matter whether Jesus was sinless or not? Even if it matters, I wonder how he could possibly remain sinless and yet be represented as "fully human, even as we are human." It is simply one of the finer points of belief in the early church that to some of us now appear rather absurd and unnecessary to faith.

Many moderate to liberal pastors and theologians no longer believe Christ's death on the cross was necessary as a condition for God's forgiveness of our sins.[53] Jesus himself taught that God had already accepted the people in his society who were treated as outcasts because they were tax collectors, prostitutes, or sinners of other varieties. He never once teaches in the Synoptic Gospels[54] that God required his death before God could pardon the sins of the people.

The truth of the matter is that Jesus' death was important because it was a defiant gesture to the religious aristocracy of his day. It was also a reminder that God considers poor men and women who cannot afford to pay priests to offer sacrifices for them as equal with the wealthy landowners and businessmen who can pay to erect churches and temples in their honor or to the honor of relatives they wish to memorialize. Jesus died shaking his fist, as it were, at the false and hypocritical assumptions people make about their own righteousness and how much God cares about it. I believe he would have scoffed at the doctrine of his own sinlessness and the false importance it has assumed as part of his role as Savior of the world.

[Handwritten margin note: His idea of why Christ was on the cross. This is a narrow view he takes - He does not know the mysteries]

By the same token, I think Joanne Rowling is enough of a scholar of world religions to scoff at the idea as well. For her, neither Dumbledore as a kind of God the father figure nor Harry as a Christ figure must be either sinless or guileless. She knows too much about the history of demanding deities and self-sacrificing saviors to be confined to the nonessentials of the Christian gospel when defining and delineating her characters. Dumbledore clearly makes mistakes—Harry Potter himself says so—and so does Harry, who becomes a sacrificial lamb only after exhausting all other options for halting the predatory Voldemort.

Harry's Proneness to Self-Sacrifice

Tales of heroic self-sacrifice of course existed before the Christian era, but few compare with the drama and intensity of the death of Jesus. It is fair to say that Jesus' willingness to go to a cross without defending himself or seeking to escape is one of the great formative motifs of Western culture, and the early Christians often modeled their lives and passions on this image.

Jaroslav Pelikan, Sterling Professor of History at Yale University, writes in his widely respected *Jesus through the Centuries: His Place in the History of Culture,*

> The followers of Jesus came very early to the conclusion that he had lived in order to die, that his death was not the interruption of his life at all but its ultimate purpose. Even by the most generous reading, the Gospels give us information about less than a hundred days in the life of Jesus; but for the last two or three days of his life, they provide a detailed, almost hour-by-hour scenario. And the

climax of the scenario is the account of Good Friday and his three hours on the cross. The Apostles' Creed and the Nicene Creed recognized this when they moved directly from his birth "from the Virgin Mary" to his crucifixion "under Pontius Pilate." What was said of the thane of Cawdor in *Macbeth* was true preeminently of Jesus: "Nothing in his life / became him like the leaving of it."[55]

Many Greeks, Romans, and Persians lived and died nobly before Jesus, but none inspired the kind of emulation that accrued from his death. "Right dying" became the order of the day. The Apostle Paul writes in his letter to the Philippians,

> Let each of you look not to your own interests, but to the interests of others. Let the same mind be in you that was in Christ Jesus, who, though he was in the form of God, did not regard equality with God as something to be exploited, but emptied himself, taking the form of a slave, being born in human likeness. And being found in human form, he humbled himself and became obedient to the point of death—even death on a cross (2:4–8).

This passage is sometimes referred to as "the kenotic passage"—from the Greek *kenosis*, "to empty"—because it describes the self-emptying of Christ. Harry Potter lives a self-emptying life. Over and over in the various volumes of the septet, he proves himself willing to lay down his life for others. In *The Sorcerer's Stone*, the first of the series, he and Ron go to Hermione's aid in a girls' bathroom when she is endangered by a 12-foot troll. The boys distract it away from her, but then it turns toward Ron. Harry does something the author calls "both very brave and very stupid"—he takes a running jump and gets his arms around the troll's neck from behind.[56] He succeeds in restraining the creature long enough for Ron to shout a curse. Clobbered by its own club, the troll staggers and falls, causing the whole room to shudder.

Later in the same novel, Harry defies Professor McGonagall's orders not to go near the dungeons where the Sorcerer's Stone is hidden. Believing Professor Snape wants to get the stone and give it to Voldemort, Harry feels compelled to beat Snape to it. "You're mad!" Ron says. "You'll be expelled!" warns Hermione. However, Harry insists that if Snape gets the stone first, Voldemort will return, and no one will be safe. "If I get caught before I can get to the stone, well, I'll have to go back to the Dursleys and wait for Voldemort to find me there; it's only dying a bit later than I would have, because I'm never going over to the Dark Side! I'm going through that trapdoor tonight and nothing you two say is going to stop me!"[57]

As Christ's death inspired his followers to risk their lives the way he did, Harry's bravery convinces Ron and Hermione to accompany him to the dungeons. Once there, they encounter several obstacles created as protection for the stone, including a gigantic vine that tries to suffocate them and a giant chessboard with enormous, living pieces. The children use magic and personal skills to get through each obstacle, but not without suffering injury and getting separated. As Ron says at the chessboard, they have to "make some sacrifices."[58]

In the inner recesses of the dungeon where he thinks he will find the Sorcerer's Stone, Harry instead finds that someone arrived before him—Professor Quirrell, whom Harry has assumed is loyal to Dumbledore. But Quirrell is hosting the weakened body of

Voldemort: when he unwraps his turban and turns around, Harry sees a terrible face, "chalk white with glaring red eyes and slits for nostrils, like a snake."[59] It is the Dark Lord himself, and he orders Quirrell to seize Harry. At the professor's touch, Harry's scar sears with pain, but Quirrell too experiences pain and even blisters when he grabs Harry.

Voldemort cries, "KILL HIM! KILL HIM!" Harry hears other voices calling his name as he blacks out. When Harry awakens, he looks into the face of Albus Dumbledore and realizes he is in the school infirmary. He learns from Dumbledore that his friends are okay, and he has been there *three days*.[60]

Three days in a coma. What does that suggest about Harry? Why didn't everyone see this in the first book of the series? A special child singled out for death; the strange happenings when he was brought to Privet Drive; his ability to speak to serpents; his incredible skill as a Seeker; his quest for the Sorcerer's Stone; his willingness to sacrifice himself for the good of others; three days in a coma.

It should have been crystal clear to anyone familiar with the story of Jesus!

Descensus ad Inferos

In *The Chamber of Secrets*, Dobby the house-elf, who belongs to Lucius Malfoy but has an affinity for Harry, insists that Harry must not return to Hogwarts for his second year because "terrible things" will happen there.[61] As a servant at the Malfoy household, Dobby has learned of steps to be taken against the "Mudbloods," or Muggle-born wizards. When Harry protests that he is not Muggle-born, Dobby continues to insist that he stay away from

Hogwarts. Of course, Harry returns to his beloved school. Later, Dobby again tries to convince Harry to leave, and Harry once more refuses, this time citing his protection of Hermione, his Muggle-born friend. Dobby says, "Harry Potter risks his own life for his friends!…So noble! So valiant! But he must save himself.…"[62]

At the Last Supper, Jesus said to his disciples, "This is my commandment, that you love one another as I have loved you. No one has greater love than this, to lay down one's life for one's friends" (John 15:12–13). Harry refuses to stay away from Hogwarts, and on more than one occasion he lays down his life for his friends—and even for a mere acquaintance. At the first meeting of the Dueling Club, Draco Malfoy accidentally conjures up a huge, venomous snake. When the fumbling Professor Lockhart attempts to make it disappear, the creature flies into the air and lands at the feet of a student named Justin Finch-Fletchley. Enraged, the snake rears to strike the terrified boy. Harry, with no thought for his own safety, immediately throws himself between Finch-Fletchley and the snake and orders it in Parseltongue, "Leave him alone!" The startled snake obeys.[63]

Harry eventually encounters another serpent in the Chamber of Secrets, a huge basilisk that ignores his Parseltongue commands. Voldemort has drawn Ron's little sister, Ginny, into the chamber below a girls' bathroom at the school, and Harry determines to go down and rescue her. After a torturous descent down a large, twisting pipe, Harry, Ron, and Lockhart find themselves "miles under the school."[64] Lockhart's faulty spell causes a collapse in the tunnel that separates him and Ron from Harry. As in *The Sorcerer's Stone*, Harry must go on alone. He follows a dark tunnel to the inner chamber, where he meets the figure of Tom Riddle. This subterranean mission into the Chamber of Secrets is strongly reminiscent of Jesus' *descensus ad inferos*, or descent into hell, popularly believed to have happened during the hours between his death on the cross and his appearances to the disciples after his resurrection.

Strictly speaking, the descent into hell is not part of the biblical tale of Christ's death. During the Middle Ages, it became an active belief in popular speculation about what happened while Jesus' body lay in the tomb provided for him by Joseph of Arimathea. We do not possess copies of the various creeds that sprang up all over Christendom in the early centuries, but we know that the descent into hell was mentioned at least as early as a Gallican creed of the sixth century, and that it was widely used as part of the Apostles' Creed by about 750 C.E.

The descent became part of medieval iconography, and numerous woodcuts from the period depict Jesus at the gates of hell, setting free the souls held captive inside. Countless sermons alluded to Jesus' descent, popularly known as the harrowing of hell, and it became the subject of many stained-glass windows of the period.

The question naturally arises: If Rowling intended Harry's descent into the secret chamber to represent this aspect of the work of Christ, why did she employ it so early in the series of Potter stories instead of reserving it for a scene at or near the end? Apparently, she was more intent on planting the clues about Harry's identification with Christ where she could—generally scattered throughout the novels—than on tipping her hand by observing a strict order of occurrence.

The truth is that the Gospels themselves were never orderly, and numerous disparities are evident among them regarding when and where certain things occurred. One of the more glaring examples is the story of Jesus' cleansing of the temple—driving out the merchants and money changers—which in the Synoptic Gospels happens during the last week of his ministry and in the Gospel of John occurs in chapter 2, near the beginning, and serves as a prelude to his ministry. Ostensibly, the placement in John is to underline a theological point the author of the Fourth Gospel attempts to get across, namely, that the expulsion of greedy businessmen from the temple was symbolic of the new broom Jesus was going to bring to Jewish religion. Rowling did only what the Gospel writers themselves were already guilty of doing—moving their material around to suit their purposes.

Practically, of course, it would have been difficult to fit Harry's descent into the chamber into the final volume of the series, after he is killed by Voldemort and before he encounters Dumbledore in the afterlife and has the discussion that makes sense of all his previous experiences. It was much easier to drop it into *The Chamber of Secrets*, where it would not prove too conspicuous a clue and end at that early stage the suspense about whether young Harry would survive his sequence of threatening experiences already bruited to stretch through seven volumes.

The Final Story

Amazingly, Harry survives encounter after encounter with Voldemort and his followers. It is part of Rowling's artfulness that she maintains suspense in volume after volume, reminiscent of old movie serials and comic book stories. Harry's engagements with evil are always fresh and exciting. In *The Prisoner of Azkaban*, Harry drives a horde of soul-sucking dementors away from his godfather

Sirius Black by casting his Patronus, which appears as a great stag representing his father James Potter. In *The Goblet of Fire*, Harry actually meets the reinvigorated Dark Lord in the cemetery where Voldemort kills Cedric Diggory and then tries to kill Harry. In *The Order of the Phoenix*, our hero battles Bellatrix Lestrange, one of Voldemort's two strongest allies, when Voldemort draws him to the Ministry of Magic using Legilimency, the art of invading another's mind. Harry then watches Dumbledore fight Voldemort, only to experience himself a brief possession by the Dark Lord. In *The Half-Blood Prince*, Harry takes part in a great battle at Hogwarts in which Dumbledore is killed. In the final volume, *The Deathly Hallows*, the repeated encounters with Voldemort come to a head in the remarkable story of Harry's own death.

This final novel deserves our scrutiny now. In *The Deathly Hallows*, we draw all the clues together in order to understand the mystery and magic of the entire series. I have spoken of the Horcruxes—the objects in which Voldemort hid pieces of himself in order to avoid death. Dumbledore and Harry search for seven of these in *The Half-Blood Prince,* and Harry and his friends Ron and Hermione continue searching in *The Deathly Hallows*. The Horcruxes include Tom Riddle's diary, a heavy golden locket that bears an S for Slytherin, Helga Hufflepuff's cup engraved with a badger, a diadem belonging to Rowena Ravenclaw, Marvolo Gaunt's ring (Gaunt was Tom Riddle's grandfather), Voldemort's snake Nagini, and Harry Potter himself. As Dumbledore explains to Severus Snape, when Voldemort killed Harry's mother Lily, the killing curse rebounded onto him, blasting apart his own soul. "Part of Lord Voldemort lives inside Harry," Dumbledore says, "and it is that which gives him the power of speech with snakes,

and a connection with Lord Voldemort's mind that he has never
understood. And while that fragment of soul, unmissed by
Voldemort, remains attached to and protected by Harry, Lord
Voldemort cannot die."[65] This is why Harry has to die—in order
that Voldemort himself can die.

Harry must die so Voldemort can die. (margin note)

I strongly suspect that Rowling had a good reason for devising
seven Horcruxes, and not four or five or six. Because she was
dealing with the evil lord himself, perhaps she was thinking about
Jesus' saying, "When the unclean spirit has gone out of a person, it
wanders through waterless regions looking for a resting place, but
not finding any, it says, 'I will return to my house from which I
came.' When it comes, it finds it swept and put in order. Then it
goes and brings seven other spirits more evil than itself, and they
enter and live there; and the last state of that person is worse than
the first" (Luke 11:24–26). There are also references in the Gospels
to seven demons being cast out of Mary Magdalene.[66]

Horcrux. Locket. (margin note)

Fascinating stories are attached to each Horcrux and its
pursuit, but one we might easily overlook involves the locket. To
get it, Dumbledore and Harry travel over a strange underground
lake (recalling the River Styx?) where they battle an army of dead
souls or Inferi. After their trouble, the locket they retrieve is
revealed as a fake, and the real one appears around the neck of
Dolores Umbridge, the Dark Lord's lieutenant at the Ministry of
Magic. Harry and Hermione manage to get the locket from
Umbridge, and when the two go to Bathilda Bagshot's house in
Godric's Hollow, where Voldemort has disguised Nagini as the old
lady, Harry feels the locket pulsing against his skin. Following his
harrowing encounter with Nagini, and reeling in pain from his
scar, Harry recalls the night years ago when Voldemort killed his

mother. This experience occurred on Christmas Eve—significant in itself—and Harry remembers seeing Voldemort point a wand at his face and hearing him say, "*Avada Kedavra!*"

At this point Harry blacks out, remaining unconscious for hours. When he wakes, his chest is burned by the locket and he has a snake wound as well. "There was a scarlet oval over his heart where the locket had burned him."[67] A scarlet oval over Harry's heart recalls the Sacred Heart of Jesus, one of the most revered signs in Christian history.

In Jewish thought, the heart was considered the center of the intellect, emotions, and understanding, the core of each person's being. Little was made of the Sacred Heart of Jesus during the first ten centuries of Christendom, but during the pietistic revivals of the eleventh and twelfth centuries, it began to play a prominent role in Christian devotionalism. The imagery representing it usually depicted a red heart pierced by a ray of light or a picture of Jesus with his heart glowing, light pouring from it, and Jesus pointing to it.

[handwritten margin note: The Sacred Heart of Jesus]

In the seventeenth century, a French Roman Catholic nun named Margaret Mary Alacoque claimed to have had a series of visions about Jesus' heart and said Jesus had commanded her to tell people about the love of his Sacred Heart. On August 31, 1670, the first Feast of the Sacred Heart was held in the Grand Seminary of Rennes, France, and the feast quickly spread to other centers of devotionalism. It soon received a permanent place on the Roman Catholic liturgical calendar nineteen days after Pentecost.

Today both Catholics and Anglicans the world over revere the Sacred Heart of Jesus as a precious symbol of God's love and their own faith, and the image of the Sacred Heart is imprinted on the title page of every book published by the Society of Jesus and painted on the walls of all their churches. Pope Benedict XVI, in a letter dated May 15, 2006, reaffirmed the importance of the Sacred Heart of Jesus and commended it to all believers as an object of their devotion. Perhaps Rowling was aware of the importance of this symbol when she wrote in *The Deathly Hallows* about the Horcrux locket that burned its image on Harry Potter's chest.

Another Set of Mysteries

The Deathly Hallows introduces us to another set of mysteries, the Hallows themselves. There are three of them: the Elder Wand, the Resurrection Stone, and the Invisibility Cloak.

Seven and three are both common biblical numbers. There are seven days of creation (Gen 1) and seven days of the week; the seventh weekday is the Sabbath day of rest (Gen 2); Pharaoh dreamed of seven good years and seven bad years (Gen 1:1–2:4); the book of Leviticus describes seven years of crop rotation (25:2–7); Jacob worked seven years for his bride Rachel and then, when he got Leah instead, he worked another seven years for Rachel (Gen 29:20, 30); one of Jesus' stories mentions seven demons (Luke 8:2); another story includes a woman with seven husbands (Mark 12:20–23); seven deacons served the early church (Acts 6:3); seven churches are addressed in the book of Revelation (Rev 1:4); Jesus said we are to forgive "seventy times seven" (Matt 18:21–22). Likewise, there are three parts of creation (heaven, world, and underworld); three members of the godhead (Father, Son, and Holy Spirit); three major feasts (Unleavened Bread, Weeks, and Booths); three divisions of the sanctuary (vestibule, nave, and inner sanctuary); and three people in Jesus' inner circle of disciples (Peter,

James, and John). Also, three-year-old animals were prized for special sacrifices (1 Sam 1:24), and Jesus was in the grave for three days.

Harry, Ron, and Hermione learn about the three Deathly Hallows from their friend Luna's father, Xenophilus Lovegood, longtime editor of *The Quibbler* and an authority on wizarding history. The quest for the Hallows, Lovegood says, begins with the Tale of the Three Brothers. Hermione remembers the story, as it appears in *The Tales of Beedle the Bard,* an old book Dumbledore left her in his will. She reads the story aloud. Three brothers use magic to cheat Death, and Death gives them rewards of their choosing for their cleverness: the oldest gets the most powerful wand in the world, the middle gets the power to recall others from death, and the youngest and humblest, fearing Death, gets an Invisibility Cloak. These three items, Lovegood says, are the Deathly Hallows.

Harry possesses the Invisibility Cloak, inherited from his father. He figures out that Dumbledore had owned the wand, and it is now buried with him in his marble tomb. Eventually he remembers the old Snitch that Dumbledore saved from Harry's first game and eventually bequeathed to him; Harry realizes the stone is inside it.

When he later removes the stone from the Snitch and turns it in his hand three times, Harry becomes aware of subtle movements on the ground. Beings that "were neither ghost nor truly flesh" glide toward him. He sees his father and mother—"You've been so brave," Lily says—and Sirius Black and Lupin. His father James asserts that they will stay with Harry "[u]ntil the very end." "We are part of you," confirms Sirius. "Invisible to anyone else." They act now as his Patronuses, accompanying him to watch over him for comfort and protection. "The dead who walked beside him through the forest were much more real to him now than the living back at the castle: Ron, Hermione, Ginny, and all the others were the ones who felt like ghosts as he stumbled and slipped toward the end of his life, toward Voldemort...."[68]

Perhaps it is a stretch, but there appears to be some similarity between this rallying of the dead around Harry and a passage in the Gospel of Matthew concerning the crucifixion: "Then Jesus cried again with a loud voice and breathed his last. At that moment the curtain of the temple was torn in two, from top to bottom. The earth shook, and the rocks were split. The tombs also were opened, and many bodies of the saints who had fallen asleep were raised. After his resurrection they came out of the tombs and entered the holy city and appeared to many" (Matt 27:50–53). There is no suggestion in Scripture that the dead who came forth from their tombs rallied around Christ. But the two incidents appear suspiciously related.

The Penultimate—and Ultimate—Encounter

Accompanied by those dearest to him, Harry Potter steps into the clearing in the woods and faces Lord Voldemort. Soon there is "a flash of green light, and everything was gone." Harry lies facedown in the silence and realizes he is naked. Looking through a bright mist, he can see clearly even without his glasses. He wishes for clothes and immediately finds warm robes. "It was extraordinary how they had appeared, just like that, the moment he had wanted them."[69]

Harry sees something fearful that looks like a small, naked child with raw red skin. He tries to comfort it, but Dumbledore appears, healthy and whole, and says it can't be helped. His former headmaster calls Harry a "wonderful boy," a "brave, brave man."

"But you're dead," said Harry.

"Oh, yes," said Dumbledore matter-of-factly.

"Then…I'm dead too?"

"Ah," said Dumbledore, smiling still more broadly. "That is the question, isn't it?"[70]

It is indeed the question. Here, in this chapter, Harry's death interests us. At the end of the series, after repeated brushes with death at the hands of Voldemort and his surrogates, Harry Potter has walked into the Dark Lord's camp alone, without using his wand, and has given his life for the lives of all the others. It is as clear a case of art imitating life—of Harry's dying as Jesus did.

Later, when Dumbledore tells Harry he must return if he wants to "finish" Lord Voldemort, Harry elects to go back. Voldemort sends Draco Malfoy's mother to examine the boy's body and see if he is really dead. Narcissa touches Harry and knows he lives, but, caring only about finding her boy Draco in the castle, she lies to Voldemort and says he is dead. "Harry Potter is dead by my hand," exults the Dark Lord, "and no man alive can threaten me now! Watch!" He shoots a *Cruciatus* curse at Harry, lifting his body "once, twice, three times into the air."[71] If it wasn't clear before, surely it is with this scene. Voldemort, the Dark Lord, has *crucified* Harry Potter.

Voldemort announces that Harry was killed "as he ran away," trying to save himself as others laid down their lives. The devil, said Jesus, is "the father of all lies" (John 8:44).

After Harry and Hermione visit Godric's Hollow, Harry receives frequent communications in his mind and through his scar from Voldemort. The visions Harry and Voldemort share have changed—"they had become blurred, shifting as though they were moving in and out of focus. Harry was just able to make out the indistinct features of an object that looked like a skull, and something like a mountain that was more shadow than substance."[72] A skull and a mountain. Perhaps this is a picture of Golgotha, the famed "place of the skull" outside of Jerusalem where Jesus died (Mark 15:22).

But what does Rowling mean by "more shadow than substance"? It sounds Platonic—as if the dream can't measure up to reality. Perhaps it is a key to the real/unreal things that will happen when Harry and Voldemort finally meet and Harry appears to die but then returns to destroy Voldemort—and later marries Ginny and raises a family, just as Ron and Hermione do.

In T. S. Eliot's *Murder in the Cathedral*, the Four Tempters say,

Man's life is a cheat and a disappointment;
All things are unreal,
Unreal or disappointing:
The Catherine wheel, the pantomime cat,
The prizes given at the children's party,
The prize awarded for the English Essay,

The scholar's degree, the statesman's decoration.
All things become less real, man passes
From unreality to unreality.[73]

It is possible that Rowling was looking at the Catherine wheel, that she saw the whole business of Harry and Voldemort's conflict as shadowy movements on a screen, while the truly real was elsewhere or otherwise—even in the humdrum, everyday existences of Harry and his friends in the "Nineteen Years Later" epilogue, or in the lives of all the Muggles who never notice the wizarding world's seismic goings-on unless they happen to spot a strange creature in a purple robe or a confluence of owls flitting about in the daytime. The same mind that created so many fantastic creatures in a mere decade and conjured up all those marvelous and often gruesome characters, both human and inhuman, with the Dickensian names, must sometimes regard life itself as a bit of movie reel gone mad on the spool, spewing out images and noises that a Zen master wouldn't bother to notice.

It is precisely in such a world where things are both real and unreal and shadows shimmer brighter than substance, where truth merges and Harry Potters and Jesus Christs become one and the same—or so nearly so that we can't tell the difference. Rowling has stirred all the facts—bits and pieces of clues—around in her mind, dropped them artfully along the leisurely, circuitous path of seven lengthy books, and then left us to figure out what is true. Though it brings us no nearer to Truth itself, we understand that Harry Potter is definitely a Christ figure and therefore had to die at the Dark Lord's hands in the final pages of the last book.

There was not, from the first—from the dream or inspiration J. K. Rowling had on that train bound for Manchester—an iota of a chance that Harry could escape this fate. He was directed by an event that happened—or didn't happen—twenty centuries in the past.

$$5$$

Our Dumbledore Who Art in Heaven

In an interview with Meredith Vieira on NBC's *Dateline* program, J. K. Rowling said that her mother's death, which occurred while she was still working on the first volume of her famous series, cast a pall over her life that she continues to confront.[74] Therefore, we catch glimpses of her ruminations about life, death, and the afterlife at various places in the narratives of her books. One of these places, I suspect, is when Harry Potter finally uses the Resurrection Stone near the end of *The Deathly Hallows*— the scenario I discuss in chapter 4 above—and Harry's parents, Sirius, and Lupin appear to him as "less substantial than living bodies, but much more than ghosts."[75]

It is not uncommon for people in grief to seek and occasionally discover some form of communion with loved ones who have passed away. A drama teacher I know says her deceased mother frequently teases her by manipulating physical objects in her home. For example, one evening, as she looked for a particular piece of jewelry, my friend turned her jewelry cask upside down on the bed but did not find the object. Later, when she returned home and lifted the cask lid to replace the jewelry she had worn, there lay the piece she had sought, prominently displayed on top of all the other jewelry. "Oh, Mother!" she exclaimed, and sat on the bed and wept. When I spaded a garden spot recently and sowed crimson clover seed in it for the winter, I found myself in strange communion with my father, who has been dead more than twenty years and used to plant crimson clover in his garden in the fall just as I did then.

Our natural eagerness for a relationship to people beyond this life may account for a noticeable fluidity between the living and the dead in all the Harry Potter books. As I point out in *God, the Devil, and Harry Potter*, Rowling invariably "treats the dead as if they are never all that far from the living, as if a very thin line divides the realms of the mortal and immortal. Her novels are peopled by innumerable ghosts as well as living creatures, and for the wizards, who are more sensitive to these matters than Muggles are, there is often some form of communication with them."[76]

In that book, I write that Rowling divides the dead into three categories: ghosts, goblins, and poltergeists. This is true of the spirits around Hogwarts. Two of the most prominent ghosts are Sir Nicholas de Mimsy-Porpington, a.k.a. Nearly Headless Nick, the resident ghost of Gryffindor Tower, who frequently tugs at an ear, pulls off his almost-but-not-quite decapitated head, and rests it on his shoulder; and Moaning Myrtle, who was murdered in one of the girls' bathrooms at the school and continues to reside there, sometimes startling younger students who haven't met her. The best-known poltergeist is Peeves, an irascible spirit who constantly behaves like a spoiled child, throwing tantrums, playing practical jokes, messing up the halls, and generally making a nuisance of himself. But these are only a few of the countless spirits that inhabit

[handwritten margin note: Relationship to the dead in the books is common. Ghosts, goblins, poltergeists]

the halls, belfries, and odd rooms of Hogwarts, mixing with the students and faculty as if their presence were the most natural thing in the world.

As a first-year student, Harry Potter is understandably startled the first time he discovers the presence of the dead: "He gasped. So did the people around him. About twenty ghosts had just streamed through the back wall. Pearly-white and slightly transparent, they glided across the room talking to one another and hardly glancing at the first years. They seemed to be arguing."[77]

But soon, Harry and his friends enjoy Nearly Headless Nick and his friends as if the ghosts are part of the student body. In *The Chamber of Secrets*, Harry and Nick walk together in the hall one day when Nick suddenly stops and Harry passes right through him, feeling as if he has stepped into an ice-cold shower. Nick then invites Harry and his friends to his five-hundredth "deathday party," to be held on Halloween in one of the castle's roomier dungeons. Harry, Ron, and Hermione attend the party, though they have second thoughts as soon as they arrive. Eerie music, revolting foods, and a cold room heighten the children's discomfort as they watch the ghosts whirl around the dance floor. Later that evening, a group of headless horsemen riding ghost horses interrupt the party, taunting Nick about his partly attached head and instigating a game of Head Hockey.[78]

With her delightful sense of comedy, Rowling must have enjoyed writing about such hijinks among the Hogwarts ghosts, knowing how much her young audiences would appreciate them. But one wonders if she didn't pause at the time to reflect on her mother's recent passing and wonder about her life after death.

The scene in *The Deathly Hallows* when Harry rubs the Resurrection Stone and summons James, Lily, Sirius, and Lupin may be of a more serious import, possibly reflecting Rowling's deeper thinking on the afterlife. These ghosts are "much more real to [Harry] than the living," and promise to stay with him to the end, whatever happens.[79] It may be that Rowling had a similar sense of assurance about her mother's presence, that her mother would see her through the ordeal of producing the entire Potter series and whatever else her life entailed.

The Key to Everything?

Rowling may have given us the key to her books in Harry and Hermione's visit to the cemetery in Godric's Hollow. As I describe in my introduction, in this scene from *The Deathly Hallows*, the two young people cross the village square and see the war memorial shift into a statue of James, Lily, and infant Harry. Then they enter the graveyard and find the graves of Dumbledore's mother and sister. Next, on a stone for Ignotus Peverell, supposedly one of the three brothers in the tale about death in Beedle's book,[80] they see the mark that symbolizes the Elder Wand, the Resurrection Stone, and the Invisibility Cloak—the three Deathly Hallows.

At last, two rows behind the graves of Dumbledore's relatives, they come to James and Lily Potter's graves. The engraving on it reads, "The last enemy that shall be destroyed is death." It is a quotation from 1 Corinthians 15:26, occurring in the middle of St. Paul's great oration about what happens when believers die. Paul's oration continues in the Scripture a few verses later:

Listen, I will tell you a mystery! We will not all die, but we will all be changed, in a moment, in the twinkling of an eye, at the last trumpet. For the trumpet will sound, and the dead will be raised imperishable, and we will be changed. For this perishable body must put on imperishability, and this mortal body must put on immortality. When this perishable body puts on imperishability, and this mortal body puts on immortality, then the saying that is written will be fulfilled: "Death has been swallowed up in victory." "Where, O death, is your victory? Where, O death, is your sting?" (1 Cor 15:51–55)

These words have been cited at literally millions of memorial services through the centuries, offering particular comfort and assurance for mourners. Perhaps Rowling heard them at her mother's funeral, either in the church or at the graveside. Maybe the words "the last enemy" continued to echo in her mind and became the seed around which she determined to construct the final novel: they would serve as the talisman for the entire series, a sign of her own brave affirmation hurled into the face of human mortality after she lost her mother.

When Harry and Hermione read the inscription on his parents' tombstone, Harry asks if the words imply an idea embraced by Death Eaters, who wish to conquer death. Hermione doesn't think so. "It means…you know…living beyond death," she says. "Living after death."[81] Finally, in a beautiful touch of sentiment, Hermione moves her wand in a circular motion to create a bouquet of Christmas roses, which Harry places on his parents' grave.

The Life, Death, and Afterlife of Albus Dumbledore

Of all the characters in Rowling's books, Albus Dumbledore is probably the most complex and, at times, the most confusing. When we meet him in the first pages of *The Sorcerer's Stone*, he is majestic and commanding, a tall, thin man with silvery hair who is obviously in charge of everything and just as obviously opposed to the Dark Lord and evil in the world. The students at Hogwarts find him wise and thoughtful. In *The Half-Blood Prince*, even Voldemort himself declares, "You are omniscient as ever, Dumbledore"[82]—a word seldom used about anyone but God.

Dumbledore and Harry often converse in the novels, and Harry's knowledge of Voldemort and his supporters is usually advanced through Dumbledore's teachings and guidance. He introduces Harry to the Pensieve or memory keeper and instructs him to value the past as much as the present and the future, for only by knowing the past may one comprehend the rest of his or her experience.

The conversation between the two of them at the end of *The Sorcerer's Stone* is typical. Harry figures Voldemort will try new ways of coming after him, and Dumbledore agrees: "He is still out there somewhere, perhaps looking for another body to share…not being truly alive, he cannot be killed."[83] Harry asks why Professor Quirrell could not touch him without being harmed.[84] Dumbledore explains,

> Your mother died to save you. If there is one thing Voldemort cannot understand, it is love. He didn't realize that love as powerful as your mother's for you leaves its own mark. Not a scar, no visible sign…to have been loved so

deeply, even though the person who loved us is gone, will give us some protection forever. It is in your skin. Quirrell, full of hatred, greed, and ambition, sharing his soul with Voldemort, could not touch you for this reason. It was agony to touch a person marked by something so good.[85]

Again, one wonders if Rowling was thinking of her mother as she wrote this passage. She must have known her mother's love continued to affect her life in positive and possibly even protective ways.

Harry also asks why Professor Snape acted in his behalf. Dumbledore explains that Snape hates Harry's father because he owes James for having saved his life; Snape thinks he can even the score by protecting Harry, and then go back to hating Harry's father's memory in peace. What about the Sorcerer's Stone? Harry wonders how he managed to possess it when he confronted Quirrell/Voldemort. Dumbledore responds with typical humor, "Ah, now...I'm glad you asked me that. It was one of my more brilliant ideas, and between you and me, that's saying something. You see, only one who wanted to *find* the Stone—find it, but not use it—would be able to get it, otherwise they'd just see themselves making gold or drinking Elixir of Life. My brain surprises even me sometimes...."[86]

Humorous. Brilliant. But Dumbledore was more. He was *generous.* At the end of *The Chamber of Secrets*, after explaining how Harry located the basilisk in the dungeon and managed to defeat the memory of Tom Riddle by stabbing his diary with a basilisk fang, Dumbledore calls for a feast and awards 200 points to

Gryffindor House. He wants the students to enjoy themselves and celebrate life, even in the midst of danger and the unknown.

He is *fair* and *just*. When he knows, in *The Prisoner of Azkaban*, that Sirius Black has been recaptured and imprisoned in a Hogwarts tower room, soon to be taken back to Azkaban prison, and that Hagrid's hippogriff Buckbeak is scheduled to be executed, he tells Harry and Hermione how to find Sirius and implies that they might save *two* lives that night. With these subtle clues, he plants in the children's minds the idea that they can rescue Buckbeak, fly him to the tower window, and let Sirius escape on him. With this plan, as with many others, Dumbledore breaks regulations imposed by the Ministry of Magic, but he cares more for fairness than rules.[87]

Dumbledore is *honest* and *open*. He tells the students at the end of *The Goblet of Fire* that the Ministry of Magic wishes to hide the fact that the Dark Lord himself killed young Cedric Diggory, but he says he disagrees with the ministry's decision. "It is my belief," he says, "that the truth is generally preferable to lies, and that any attempt to pretend that Cedric died as the result of an accident, or some sort of blunder of his own, is an insult to his memory."[88] Dumbledore acknowledges that they all face "dark and difficult times," but they are better off knowing and facing the truth than believing a lie. "Remember Cedric," the headmaster says. "Remember, if the time should come when you have to make a choice between what is right and what is easy, remember what happened to a boy who was good, and kind, and brave, because he strayed across the path of Lord Voldemort. Remember Cedric Diggory."[89]

Dumbledore is also *humble*. In *The Order of the Phoenix*, he confesses to Harry that Sirius Black died at the Ministry of Magic because Dumbledore had kept information from Harry. If he had told Harry everything he knew, the boy would not have been tricked into going to the ministry that night, thus putting Sirius in danger when he came to rescue his godson. "Harry, I owe you an explanation," Dumbledore says. "An explanation of an old man's mistakes. For I see now that what I have done, and not done, with regard to you, bears all the hallmarks of the failings of age. Youth cannot know how age thinks and feels. But old men are guilty if they forget what it was to be young...and I seem to have forgotten lately...."[90]

Dumbledore insists that it is time to tell Harry everything. He explains why he placed Harry with the Dursleys, in a home he despised: because Petunia Dursley is Harry's mother's sister and therefore from her bloodline. Because of the blood tie, while Harry lives in Petunia's home, Dumbledore is able to place a charm on his life so that Voldemort cannot reach him. Dumbledore admits that keeping the truth from Harry was a mistake. "I cared more for your happiness than your knowing the truth," he says, "more for your peace of mind than my plan, more for your life than the lives that might be lost if the plan failed. In other words, I acted exactly as Voldemort expects we fools who love to act."[91] In the next novel, *The Half-Blood Prince*, Dumbledore alludes again to his fallibility, admitting that he can be wrong. "In fact," he says, "being—forgive me—rather cleverer than most men, my mistakes tend to be correspondingly huger."[92]

But for all his faults, Dumbledore is *loving*. Unlike Voldemort, he loves others. In one way, this love is his most important shortcoming as a wizard, because it sometimes affects his judgment, particularly concerning Harry's innocence. Yet he believes in the power of love more than in any other kind of power, and he honors that singular power in Harry Potter.

When Harry and Dumbledore discuss how Voldemort has hidden parts of himself in several Horcruxes, Harry asks if this means the Dark Lord can be killed by the one who finds and destroys all the Horcruxes. Dumbledore thinks so, but he reminds Harry that Voldemort is such an unusually resourceful wizard that it will take "uncommon skill and power" to kill such a figure.[93]

> "But I haven't got uncommon skill and power," said Harry, before he could stop himself.
>
> "Yes, you have," said Dumbledore firmly. "You have a power that Voldemort has never had. You can—"
>
> "I know!" said Harry impatiently. "I can *love!*" It was only with difficulty that he stopped himself adding, "Big deal!"
>
> …"It is essential that you understand this!" said Dumbledore…; Harry had never seen him so agitated. "By attempting to kill you, Voldemort himself singled out the remarkable person who sits here in front of me, and gave him the tools for the job! …You are protected, in short, by your ability to *love!*"[94]

In this, the next-to-last book in the series, Dumbledore decides to give Harry special lessons to prepare him for combat with the Dark Lord. Several of these are in the form of visits—via the Pensieve—to the past. Then, when Harry understands about the Horcruxes, Dumbledore takes him on a dangerous journey to a great underground lake, where he thinks one of the Horcruxes is hidden. On an island in the middle of the lake, they find a stone basin full of a strange emerald liquid. A locket that bears an "S," which Dumbledore believes is the Horcrux, lies at the bottom of the basin. When they realize they can't reach through the liquid, since it becomes solid to the touch, Dumbledore decides that he must drink it completely, no matter how much he wishes to stop. He insists on being the one to drink "[b]ecause I am much older, much cleverer, and much less valuable."[95]

Drinking the liquid proves excruciating, and Harry has to force his headmaster to keep going until the older man cries, "Kill me!" and loses consciousness. When Dumbledore revives, he grabs the locket. The two make their way out of the deadly cave, with Harry comforting a seriously weakened Dumbledore, who responds, "I am not worried, Harry.... I am with you."[96]

Upon their return to Hogwarts, the two encounter Death Eaters, including Draco Malfoy, whom Voldemort has instructed to kill Dumbledore. "Draco, Draco, you are not a killer," [97] Dumbledore tells the boy, causing Draco to hesitate. While Draco debates with Dumbledore, Professor Snape appears. Despite Dumbledore's pleas for mercy, Snape raises his wand and blasts Dumbledore into the air, where he hangs briefly before falling "like a great rag doll, over the battlements and out of sight."[98] Dumbledore—God the Father?—is dead. He is, finally, *finite* and *limited.*

The Inevitable Question

We are left with a piercing question. If Dumbledore is finite—if he admits making mistakes, if he doesn't know he has found a fake locket, if he is severely weakened by the quest for the

Horcrux, if he begs Severus Snape for mercy, if he dies from Snape's *Avada Kedavra* curse, if he is truly *gone*—then how can he by any stretch of the imagination represent God the Father?

The question becomes even harder to answer after the final book, *The Deathly Hallows*, for in the scene between Harry and Dumbledore in the afterlife, we learn that Dumbledore was at least slightly less than admirable as a young man. He and a close friend, Gellert Grindelwald, actually conspired to gain power by assembling the three Hallows and to rule over the Muggle world. "I was selfish, Harry," Dumbledore confesses, "more selfish than you, who are a remarkably selfless person, could possibly imagine."[99]

After severe family trauma in which his sister Ariana was attacked by three Muggle boys and rendered unable to perform magical acts, Dumbledore resented having to care for her once their mother died. When Grindelwald came to Godric's Hollow, he and young Dumbledore connected: "You cannot imagine how his ideas caught me, Harry, inflamed me. Muggles forced into subservience. We wizards triumphant. Grindelwald and I, the glorious young leaders of the revolution."[100]

Dumbledore wasn't without scruples, even in his early days. He assuaged his conscience by telling himself everyone would be better off in a different world—even the Muggles. Rowling's novels emphasize this point repeatedly: any revolution would be "for the general good." "The general good" is likely a reference to one of the most famous schools of thought in British ethical history, known as Utilitarianism. Elaborated by an attorney named Jeremy Bentham (1748–1832) and a one-term parliamentarian named John Stuart Mill (1806–1873), the philosophy held that legislators should always seek to provide "the greatest happiness for the greatest number." It asserted that such a principle was not only defensible on moral grounds but was actually achievable by legislators capable of assessing what would make people happy and of measuring the amount of happiness their actions would provide.

For Dumbledore and Grindelwald, the Deathly Hallows offered a means to the noble end for the general good. The Hallows—especially the Resurrection Stone—fascinated them both. Dumbledore realized much later that Grindelwald wished to use it to bring back an army of Inferi, dead souls on evil's side, while Dumbledore himself wanted to bring back his parents and thus lift the responsibility of his sister from his shoulders. Dumbledore's brother Aberforth shouted truths at the young men that they didn't want to hear. Grindelwald lost control and a fight ensued. Curses flew everywhere, and one struck and killed Ariana. No one was ever certain whose curse was responsible.

These events, as Dumbledore explains to Harry in the afterlife, took place many years ago. Dumbledore didn't see Grindelwald again. He heard rumors about him—that he had procured a wand of immense power and held great authority in Europe. Meanwhile, Dumbledore was offered the post of Minister of Magic, the highest honor in wizardry. He refused to take it, however, explaining to Harry that he had learned he "was not to be trusted with power." When Harry insists that Dumbledore would have been "much better" than other ministers, Dumbledore responds, "Would I? …I am not so sure. I had proven, as a very young man, that power was my weakness and my temptation."[101]

Years later, Dumbledore discovered the Resurrection Stone hidden in a ring at the Gaunts' home—"the Hallow I had craved most of all, though in my youth I had wanted it for very different reasons"—and, forgetting that Voldemort had made the ring a Horcrux, tried it on. For a second, he says to Harry, he thought he might see his dead sister, his mother, and his father and tell them how sorry he was. Instead, the curse reverberated through his body and left his hand blasted and useless. He realized his unworthiness to unite the three Hallows.

Earlier in the final novel, Harry expresses to Hermione his resentment of Dumbledore, whom he believes intentionally made his task difficult: "his fury broke over him now like lava, scorching him inside, wiping out every other feeling.... Dumbledore had left them to grope in the darkness, to wrestle with unknown and undreamed-of terrors, alone and unaided."[102] Harry has had enough: "Look what he asked from me, Hermione! ...Risk your life, Harry! And again! And again! And don't expect me to explain everything, just trust me blindly, trust that I know what I'm doing, trust me even though I don't trust you! Never the whole truth! Never!"[103] It was the sort of thing Jesus might have said of his heavenly Father.

Of course, in the afterlife, Harry finally has a chance to ask Dumbledore why he withheld essential information from him for so long. Dumbledore explains, "I was scared that, if presented outright with the facts about those tempting objects, you might seize the Hallows as I did, at the wrong time, for the wrong reasons. If you laid hands on them, I wanted you to possess them safely. You are the true master of death, because the true master does not seek to run away from Death. He accepts that he must die, and understands that there are far, far worse things in the living world than dying."[104] As we know from our own journeys of faith, no higher power can give us all the answers. We have to find them for ourselves—or learn to forge ahead without them. Such wonderings and doubts are part of the journey, part of what Jesus himself endured as he stumbled toward the cross.

This is Dumbledore fully revealed. In some ways, he is a broken wizard, one who regrets his past actions and looks upon himself as a failure. But he *does* shelter and train Harry Potter. He cultivates the Boy Who Lived, and in the final analysis enables him to win over Voldemort—though at this point in the novel that victory is yet to come. Dumbledore loves Harry Potter.

Is Dumbledore really God the Father, as I suggest in *God, the Devil, and Harry Potter?* His name is an old British word for "bumblebee" and is equivalent to the Scottish *cockchafer*, which means "a May bug or beetle." The beetle was sacred in ancient Egyptian religion—one of Rowling's majors at Exeter University was in Classics or Ancient Mythology (the other was in French)—and the Khepera, or scarab beetle, was thought to roll the sun into place each day the way a dung beetle methodically rolled up balls of dung in the sand. Blue or green beetles were enclosed in almost every Egyptian sarcophagus. These facts become particularly interesting when we recall the first scene in *The Sorcerer's Stone*, at the start of the Potter saga, in which Professor McGonagall waits for Harry's arrival outside the Dursley home in the form of a cat. The cat was also significant in Egyptian mythology and was thought to be related to the moon because of the way the moon reflects in the pupils of a cat's eyes (Dumbledore sees McGonagall's eyes in the dark shadows at the end of the Dursleys' street). In some Egyptian tales, a goddess named Bast assumes the form of a cat and sits with her foot on the head of the reptile Night—the enemy of the sun—until Khepera rolls the sun back into place each morning.

These connections aren't the same thing as announcing that Dumbledore is the deity of the Judeo-Christian religion, but they are surely clues to his significance as a special figure in the Harry Potter books. If he isn't the one who makes the sun come up, he is at least the single most important person in Harry's life—serving as his mentor and protector, and, in the end, the one who waits to greet him in the afterlife after Voldemort kills him. If Harry Potter is truly a Christ figure, about which I have little doubt, then Dumbledore is most reasonably the corresponding figure of his heavenly Father.

Of course, he doesn't exactly match traditional understandings of the Judeo-Christian God. He is finite, fallible, and not completely omniscient. He makes mistakes—especially as a young man—and admits to his early eagerness for power and revenge. He is not unchangeable. He has evolved, over the years, from a self-absorbed, ambitious young wizard into a thoughtful, kindly, and loving old man, eager to secure the happiness of all.

But is this not in some ways exactly the learning and experience curve through which Christians view the journey of their God? The God of the Old Testament is remote (he will not even show his face to Moses, the greatest leader of the Israelites), jealous ("I the Lord your God am a jealous God, punishing children for the iniquity of parents, to the third and the fourth generation"), vengeful (frequently smiting those who cross or disregard him), and petty (it takes little to set him off). The God of the New Testament, whose character evolves considerably through the later prophets, the psalmists, and the intertestamental period, is loving, forgiving, and eager for reconciliation, not vengeance. He loves the world so much that "he gave his only Son, so that everyone who believes in him may not perish but may have everlasting life" (John 3:16). St. Paul speaks of the "kindness and forbearance and patience" of God that are meant to lead people to repentance (Rom 2:4), and of God's sending the Spirit of his Son into our hearts, crying, "Abba! Father!" so that we are no longer God's slaves or servants but rather his children (Gal 4:6–7). God's whole aim, says the author of the letter to the Ephesians, is to break down the dividing wall between peoples—especially the Jews and Gentiles—and therefore he "abolished the law with its commandments and ordinances, that he might create in himself one new humanity in place of the two, thus making peace, and might reconcile both groups to God in one body through the cross, thus putting to death that hostility through it" (Eph 2:15–16). Isn't this precisely the evolution that occurs in Dumbledore—from self-absorption and self-aggrandizement to loving kindness, forgiveness, and inclusiveness?

If Rowling is a "creative theologian," given to fantastic images and fluid conceptions, this tendency is hardly unwarranted by the contemporary theological situation, where traditional under-standings of God have broken down for most people. Currently, there is so much speculation and difference of opinion among various Christian groups that no one theologian has been able to speak with any kind of authority since the great Karl Barth and Paul Tillich half a century ago. More freedom of thought exists in Christian circles today—at least in those not bogged down in fundamentalism—mirroring more closely the early years of the church when, as the many "gospels" found in the Nag Hammadi discovery in 1956 indicate, there was an absolute wildness of expression and creativity in the many branches of Christendom. In fact, the most important stream of theological inquiry today is probably the one that explores the mutual relations between religion and science, and how the discoveries of quantum physics invite a rapprochement between the two. The inevitable result of all this will be a new Christianity in which most of the biblical account is regarded as stories or mythology of the same kind as those that once adorned Greek and Roman religion—that is, folk tales and history embellished to support a point of view or way of life that itself is now in danger of becoming extinct.

No, Dumbledore does not conform exactly to traditional images of God the Father. But yes, he resembles many of those images. If the formation of the Christian story is regarded as the most important aspect of Jesus' concept of divine Fatherhood, so that it became the matrix out of which Western civilization as we know it was to spring, then yes, Dumbledore nicely fulfills the role of God the Father. After all, he, more than any other character in Rowling's saga, is responsible for the molding and shaping of Harry Potter, the Boy Who *Lives*, the Chosen One who finally defeats the evil Lord Voldemort and for the time being saves the world.

Certainly, Dumbledore bungles things from time to time. Didn't the actual God the Father, the deity of Judeo-Christian religion, do the same? And of course Dumbledore is in some way dependent on his young savior—even more than Harry is dependent on him. Hasn't that come to be true of the God of the Christian religion? Why else do people worship Jesus and lift their arms to him in praise and adoration if he is not their God and has not replaced God the Father in their understanding and affection?

Maybe Rowling sees Christianity from a different viewpoint than the one most Christians have. As she began writing her saga, she was a single mother, virtually alone while raising her daughter, culturally familiar with the church but not integrally involved in it, studying ancient mythology and looking at religion as a sociocultural phenomenon through the ages, and living abroad and watching people being religious and superstitious in a foreign language. She is bound to have a different take on life and religion and to process it through her extraordinarily creative mind.

Her God the Father *would* look different from most people's, wouldn't he? He might be more human, more fragile, more prone to error than the traditional God. Yet, the end product—redemption from evil, harmony in the world, people dwelling in love and peace—is the same.

If Harry Potter *is* Christ—I believe we are left with no options regarding that fact—then Dumbledore has *got* to be God the Father.

Our Dumbledore who art in heaven…

6

RESURRECTION AND THE LIFE EVERLASTING

As J. K. Rowling told Meredith Vieira in the *Dateline* interview, her mother's death before the completion of the first volume of the Harry Potter series had a great impact on her thinking and contributed substantially to the shaping of the entire saga.[105] As discussed in chapter 5, the influence of this important event is evident throughout the series—even in book one, *Harry Potter and the Sorcerer's Stone*, we witness the way ghosts intrude upon the living in the halls of Hogwarts—and nowhere does it appear more prominently than in the final chapters of the last book, *Harry Potter and the Deathly Hallows*, where Rowling's idea of heaven and the manner in which dead and living souls continue to interact with one another is presented.

Basically, we can note five things about the relationship between the dead and the living in the Harry Potter series:

1. The fascinating fluidity with which ghosts move in and out among the living, as seen in the casual way Nearly Headless Nick and his friends frolic through the halls and passageways of Hogwarts and even invite Harry, Ron, and Hermione to Nick's "deathday party."

2. The way loved ones continue to be involved in a person's thinking and life situations after death, as represented by James and Lily's continuing care for their son Harry, as well as Sirius Black's and Remus Lupin's ongoing support of Harry.

3. The continuing fellowship of those who are reunited in the afterlife, as exemplified in the warm greeting Dumbledore extends to Harry when he joins him in the heavenly scene.

4. The luminous clarity that comes to minds after death—an ability to see things in their true perspective and understand everything that has occurred with a new and more satisfying penetration.

5. The general sense of love that survives death and characterizes saints in the afterlife.

One suspects that Rowling, with her febrile imagination, entertained various thoughts of the way the dead and the living continue to interact after loved ones pass, and believed that her deceased mother was somehow present with her in the labor and achievement of her writing, as well as in the raising of her young daughter. She probably wondered a great deal about the afterlife and what it is like, mulling over church doctrine and new age thought until she arrived at a comfortable acceptance of some personal doctrine on the matter. Above all, it seems that she realized love is the most important emotion in human existence—though it may not be confined to humans—and that it not only triumphs over death but continues to work in our lives to bring us to the highest levels of consciousness suggested by both religion and philosophy.

"Washed in the Blood"

In the general fluidity of life and death imagined by Rowling, Harry Potter's resurrection from death is not a difficult feat. Harry dies—or appears to die—when he first offers himself to Voldemort as the sacrificial lamb for the lives of the others being killed or destroyed by Voldemort and his supporters. Voldemort expects him, insisting, "Potter will come to me. I know his weakness, you see, his one great flaw. He will hate watching the others struck down around him, knowing that it is for him that it happens. He will want to stop it at any cost. He will come."[106] It is also what Harry understands and chooses to do: "Harry understood at last that he was not supposed to survive. His job was to walk calmly into Death's welcoming arms. Along the way, he was to dispose of Voldemort's remaining links to life, so that when at last he flung himself across Voldemort's path, and did not raise a wand to defend himself, the end would be clean, and the job that ought to have been done in Godric's Hollow would be finished. Neither would live, neither could survive."[107]

Is it a real death, or is Harry merely stunned by Voldemort's first curse? Scholars and quibblers still debate whether Jesus was actually dead or had only passed out when he was removed from the cross and placed in a borrowed tomb. The writer of the Fourth Gospel later went to great lengths to assure his readers that Jesus was truly dead. Jesus not only spent three hours or more nailed to a crossbeam and hanging over a crowd of detractors, but he also had a spear thrust into his side by a Roman soldier to make sure he was dead (John 19:34). But scholars often discount the Fourth Gospel in conversations about such matters, believing it was concocted to represent certain viewpoints and answer the Gnostics, who argued that physical death and resurrection were beside the point for them. New Testament professors continue to take sides over whether the man taken down from the middle cross that day had actually and definitively died or was merely stunned and later revived in the coolness of the tomb. Perhaps Rowling was aware of this quarrel and deliberately left the matter hazy in her account of Harry Potter's death or *apparent* death.

In some kind of afterlife—either a real afterlife or a dream while he is in a coma—Harry meets Dumbledore and has the long conversation that both clarifies many previous mysteries for him and propels him back into his life-and-death battle with Voldemort. Harry is surprised to see Dumbledore, since he has assumed his headmaster died. Now that he encounters Dumbledore, does that mean he, Harry, is dead too?

> "Ah," said Dumbledore, smiling still more broadly. "That is the question, isn't it? On the whole, dear boy, I think not."
>
> They looked at each other, the old man still beaming.
>
> "Not?" repeated Harry.
>
> "Not," said Dumbledore.
>
> "But…" Harry raised his hand instinctively toward the lightning scar. It did not seem to be there. "But I should have died—I didn't defend myself! I meant to let him kill me!"
>
> "And that," said Dumbledore, "will, I think, have made all the difference."[108]

Exactly what difference? Here is where Rowling hedges, shading the answer so finely that it is not entirely possible to tell what she intended. I think she did it purposefully, not inadvertently. She *wanted* to leave the waters murky. Perhaps she felt it incumbent on her to do so because no one quite understands such matters, and she didn't feel qualified to be *too* certain about them.

The real point is that Harry did the right thing in letting Voldemort kill him—or in assuming Voldemort killed him, Dumbledore appears elated by the result of the encounter. Happiness radiates from him "like light, like fire. Harry had never seen the man so utterly, so palpably content."[109] In permitting Voldemort to kill him, Harry allows the Dark Lord to kill the portion of himself that resides in Harry, the seventh Horcrux. Harry recalls the time described in *The Goblet of Fire* when Wormtail baptized Voldemort with some of Harry's blood in the cauldron.[110] Dumbledore concurs, saying, "He took your blood and rebuilt his living body with it! Your blood in his veins, Harry, Lily's protection inside both of you! He tethered you to life while he lives!" Their relationship began even earlier than that, of course. Dumbledore explains to Harry exactly what happened when Voldemort tried to kill him as a baby. Something of Voldemort got into Harry then, so that Harry became "the Horcrux he never meant to make."[111]

Why does Rowling focus so much in this conversation on Harry's blood being given to Voldemort as detailed in *The Goblet of Fire*? Isn't it enough that Voldemort has now killed the part of himself that hid within Harry? Or is this Rowling's gesture toward the Christian emphasis on the blood of Christ as the sacrifice for the sins of the world? Perhaps Rowling thought no portrait of

Harry as Jesus would be complete without a reference to the shedding of blood. Certainly, early Christianity emphasized the blood—in the letter to the Hebrews especially, which offers a lengthy comparison of Jesus with the old blood sacrifices in the temple (see especially Heb 8:11–10:22)—and the blood became a central motif in the Mass, particularly in the Middle Ages, when the doctrine of transubstantiation finally decreed that the wine used in the Lord's Supper actually becomes the real blood of Jesus. If this seems like overkill in the Potter story—no pun intended—it is necessary for a complete identification of Harry with Christ.

In some pockets of Christianity, the blood metaphor is still highly regarded. Some worshipers sing seemingly endless hymns about being washed in the blood, being saved by the blood, and the preciousness of the blood. One such hymn, by Robert Lowry, begins, "What can wash away my sin? / Nothing but the blood of Jesus." Another, by the English poet William Cowper, declares, "There is a fountain filled with blood / Drawn from Emmanuel's veins; / And sinners, plunged beneath that flood, / Lose all their guilty stains." For those Christians, Harry Potter could not possibly serve as a Christ figure without some emphasis on the blood he shed to save others.

The Strange "Child"

One of the more curious aspects of Harry's afterlife visit with Dumbledore is the existence of a creature that makes odd gurgling noises. "It had the form of a small, naked child, curled on the ground, its skin raw and rough, flayed-looking, and it lay shuddering under a seat where it had been left, unwanted, stuffed out of sight, struggling for breath."[112] The creature continues to disturb Harry, who feels as if he ought to comfort it, though it repulses him. Dumbledore, however, assures Harry, "There is no help possible."[113] At last, when their discussion draws to a close, Harry glances again "at the raw-looking thing that trembled and choked in the shadow beneath the distant chair." Dumbledore counsels, "Do not pity the dead, Harry.... Pity the living, and, above all, those who live without love. By returning, you may ensure that fewer souls are maimed, fewer families are torn apart. If that seems to you a worthy goal, then we say good-bye for the present."[114]

Surely the repulsive creature symbolizes something other than itself, something Rowling wants Harry and the reader to understand. One's first impulse may be to regard it as a discarded fetus, an embryo, or a newborn child rejected by its parents. Or is it something from Harry himself—his unrequited infancy, when he was torn away from his parents, perhaps, or his own childish innocence, now raw and sensitive after all he has endured? Could it represent the children of the world living and dying of poverty and disease in troubled places like Darfur, Ethiopia, and the Middle East or in the back streets of London, Mumbai, and New York?

Maybe it's the little part of Voldemort that has been lodged in Harry since his infancy, and is now blasted out of Harry by the *Avada Kedavra* curse he experienced. Or perhaps it is Voldemort's soul itself. In *The Goblet of Fire*, when Wormtail carries the shriveled soul of Voldemort to their meeting with Harry Potter and Cedric Diggory in the cemetery at Godric's Hollow, Rowling provides this description of the Dark Lord: "The thing Wormtail had been carrying had *the shape of a crouched human child*, except that Harry had never seen anything less like a child. *It was hairless and scaly-looking, a dark, raw, reddish black.* Its arms and legs were *thin and feeble,* and its face—no child alive ever had a face like that—flat and snakelike, with gleaming red eyes."[115]

Surely the similarity of the two descriptions is not accidental; perhaps the pitiable infant Harry sees in the afterlife is the same one he beheld in the cemetery at Godric's Hollow. If this is true, then Rowling here provides a glimpse into her idea of what becomes of the souls of terrible people in the life beyond death: they revert to the weakest, most ineffectual stage of their miserable existences. Augustine believed that the souls of the redeemed continue to exist at their happiest, most fulfilling stages of being. Rowling expresses the opposite opinion about the souls of the wicked, that they suffer in the afterlife as weak, undeveloped shadows of their former selves—in short, that they continue in a hellish kind of limbo.

Harry Redivivus

Again, Rowling is artfully vague in this afterlife chapter called "King's Cross." Even her description of Harry's resurrection is almost nonchalant. After their lengthy discussion, Harry asks Dumbledore,

> "I've got to go back, haven't I?"
> "That is up to you."
> "I've got a choice?"
> "Oh yes." Dumbledore smiled at him. "We are in King's Cross, you say? I think that if you decided not to go back, you would be able to…let's say…board a train."
> "And where would it take me?"
> "On," said Dumbledore simply.[116]

I expect Rowling packed some irony into the title of this chapter. It refers, at the literal level, to King's Cross Station on the Underground in London, the station where Hogwarts students depart from platform 9 3/4 on their journey to the magical school. When Harry first arrives in this afterlife location, he notices that it resembles a big underground station. However, considering the situation and what he and Dumbledore discuss in the chapter, I suspect Rowling was perhaps also thinking about Jesus and his cross—the *King's* cross—and how that cross involved not only dying but returning to life for the sake of others.

For Harry, this station is obviously a happy, delightful place. When he arrives there, he observes a bright mist everywhere—maybe a sign of life and growth. He lies on a white floor that is neither hot nor cold, just a flat place to be. He wears no glasses and can see clearly without them. He feels no pain anywhere. When he wishes for clothing, it appears and he dons it. The scene is like a pleasant, unthreatening dream. He is reunited with his beloved Dumbledore there, and Dumbledore smiles frequently and tells Harry how well he has done. They talk about all the things Harry hasn't understood, and everything becomes clear for him. It is difficult for Harry to leave, as "he knew that he was heading back to pain and the fear of more loss." "Tell me one last thing," he says before going back. "Is this real? Or has this been happening inside my head?"[117]

There it is—Rowling's artistry. When Jean-Paul Sartre encountered something similar to this scene in the plays of Jean Gênet, Sartre said Gênet made his audiences "look at the whirligig."[118] Rowling does that to us, taunting us with the possibility that none of what she writes about really happens; it may all be a dream.

Dumbledore once more smiles at Harry as the mist descends again. "Of course it is happening inside your head, Harry," he says, "but why on earth should that mean that it is not real?"[119]

I am reminded of George Bernard Shaw's Saint Joan, when Robert de Baudricourt says to Joan that the voices of God she keeps hearing, which tell her how to lead the French to victory over the English, do not come from God but from her imagination. "Of course," Joan answers cheerfully. "That is how the messages of God come to us."[120]

When Harry returns, he is lying facedown on the ground where Voldemort's killing curse left him. Voldemort makes a spectacle of Harry's body, performing the *Cruciatus* curse and lifting him "once, twice, three times into the air" while his evil audience laughs. Then he orders Hagrid to carry the body into the castle, for he wants Harry's friends and supporters to see their hero now. "Harry Potter is dead," Voldemort announces. "He was killed as he ran away, trying to save himself while you lay down your lives for him. We bring you his body as proof that your hero is gone."[121]

Voldemort promises to spare them if they will bow down to him. Feigning death, Harry hears Hagrid's sobs and the screams of his professors and friends, and he wants to call out to them, to reassure them that he isn't dead. The parade halts, and Harry's body is laid on the grass. Voldemort repeats his lie that Harry was killed sneaking away, trying to save himself.

The repetition of his message highlights another unmistakable reference to the crucifixion of Jesus:

It was nine o'clock in the morning when they crucified him. The inscription of the charge against him read, "The King of the Jews." And with him they crucified two bandits, one on his right and one on his left. Those who passed by derided him, shaking their heads and saying, "Aha! You who would destroy the temple and build it in three days, save yourself, and come down from the cross!" In the same way the chief priests, along with the scribes, were also mocking him among themselves and saying, "He saved others; he cannot save himself. Let the Messiah, the King of Israel, come down from the cross now, so that we may see and believe." (Mark 15:25–32)

At this point, Harry peers through cracked eyelids as Neville charges Voldemort and then, when the Dark Lord invites him to join the Death Eaters, adamantly refuses and cries, "Dumbledore's Army!"[122] In the ensuing chaos, Harry quickly throws his Invisibility Cloak over himself and joins the battle as many things happen at once.

The charging centaurs were scattering the Death Eaters, everyone was fleeing the giants' stamping feet, and nearer and nearer thundered the reinforcements that had come from who knew where; Harry saw great winged creatures soaring around the heads of Voldemort's giants, thestrals and Buckbeak the hippogriff scratching at their eyes while Grawp punched and pummeled them; and now the wizards, defenders of Hogwarts and Death Eaters alike, were being forced back into the castle. Harry was shouting jinxes and curses at any Death Eater he could see, and they crumpled, not knowing what or who had hit them, and their bodies were trampled by the retreating crowd.[123]

Rowling has created an apocalyptic scene that sounds like a description straight out of the Revelation of St. John: "And war broke out in heaven; Michael and his angels fought against the dragon. The dragon and his angels fought back, but they were defeated, and there was no longer any place for them in heaven. The great dragon was thrown down, that ancient serpent, who is called the Devil and Satan, the deceiver of the whole world—he was thrown down to the earth, and his angels were thrown down with him" (Rev 12:7–9).

The battle moves into the castle itself, with more and more allies storming up the front steps. Friends and family members of students appear, as do centaurs, house-elves, and shopkeepers and homeowners of the village of Hogsmeade. In the Great Hall, Voldemort slays people right and left, with Bellatrix fighting fifty yards away from him. At that moment, Harry pulls off the Invisibility Cloak, spurring screams of "Harry!" and "He's alive!" Quickly, Harry puts a protective spell on the rest of the crowd and faces his enemy.

Voldemort and the Boy Who Lived begin to circle, eyeing and threatening each other. Harry insists that Voldemort can kill no one else this evening because of what Harry has done, protecting the others as Harry's mother protected him. "'Is it love again?' said Voldemort, his snake's face jeering. 'Dumbledore's favorite solution, *love,* which he claimed conquered death, though love did not stop him falling from the tower and breaking like an old waxwork? *Love,* which did not prevent me stamping out your

Mudblood mother like a cockroach, Potter—and nobody seems to love you enough to run forward this time and take my curse. So what will stop you dying now when I strike?'"[124]

During their parry of words, Harry reveals that Voldemort's wand, the Elder Wand, will not work properly for him because he did not take it from its rightful owner by battle. Then Harry explains that Severus Snape, whom Voldemort has trusted, was a double agent all along, serving Dumbledore. Harry even suggests that Voldemort try for remorse. But of course, that is not Voldemort's intention.

At last the two discharge their curses at one another.

> The bang was like a cannon blast, and the golden flames that erupted between them, at the dead center of the circle they had been treading, marked the point where the spells collided. Harry saw Voldemort's green jet meet his own spell, saw the Elder Wand fly high, dark against the sunrise, spinning across the enchanted ceiling like the head of Nagini, spinning through the air toward the master it would not kill, who had come to take full possession of it at last. And Harry, with the unerring skill of the Seeker, caught the wand in his free hand as Voldemort fell backward, arms splayed, the slit pupils of the scarlet eyes rolling upward. Tom Riddle hit the floor with a mundane finality, his body feeble and shrunken, the white hands empty, the snakelike face vacant and unknowing. Voldemort was dead, killed by his own rebounding curse, and Harry stood with two wands in his hand, staring down at his enemy's shell.[125]

Here Rowling offers a description of the eschatological moment, the death of the Dark Lord and the triumph of Harry Potter, the Boy Who Lived.

The witnesses scream and roar in excitement, and at that moment "the fierce new sun dazzled the windows." A new day has come. *It is Easter morning at Hogwarts!* Ron and Hermione reach Harry first, followed closely by other dearly loved ones. "Harry could not hear a word that anyone was shouting, nor tell whose hands were seizing him, pulling him, trying to hug some part of him, hundreds of them pressing in, all of them determined to touch the Boy Who Lived, the reason it was over at last."[126]

As the sun continues to rise, filling the Great Hall with light, Harry becomes "an indispensable part" of everyone's jubilation, everyone's need to celebrate and rejoice. "They wanted him there with him, their leader and symbol, *their savior and their guide*, and that he had not slept, that he craved the company of only a few of them, seemed to occur to no one."[127]

Pandemic harmony exists in the tumult, like that at Pentecost for the early Christians, because "nobody was sitting according to House anymore: All were jumbled together, teachers and pupils, ghosts and parents, centaurs and house-elves, and Firenze [the centaur] lay recovering in a corner, and Grawp [the giant] peered in through a smashed window, and people were throwing food into his laughing mouth."[128] For them as for the first Christians, their unspeakable joy melts all barriers, and they are completely united in their love and delight in their savior, Harry.

But Rowling wasn't finished when she penned these descriptions of the aftermath of Harry's victory. Harry then looks around and sees families reuniting everywhere, and, "finally, he saw the two whose company he craved most"—Ron and Hermione, his faithful lieutenants in the long war against Voldemort. "It's me," he says, crouching down between them.[129] Similar are these words from the Gospel of John: "When evening came, his disciples went down to the sea, got into a boat, and started across the sea to Capernaum. It was now dark, and Jesus had not yet come to them. The sea became rough because a strong wind was blowing. When they had rowed about three or four miles, they saw Jesus walking on the sea and coming near the boat, and they were terrified. But he said to them, 'It is I; do not be afraid.'" (John 6:16–21)

The sea stories in the Gospels—this one in John and those in the Synoptics as well—are not mere biographical tidbits. They are actually *post-resurrection stories*, images of the risen Christ appearing to his disciples when they were threatened by a storm. Also, in the Gospel of John, the phrase "It is I" or "I am"—*ego eimi* in the Greek—echoes again and again, as Jesus says, "I am the bread of life" (John 6:35), "I am the light of the world" (John 8:12; 9:5), "I am the gate for the sheep" (John 10:7), "I am the good shepherd" (John 10:11), "I am the resurrection and the life" (John 11:25), "I am the way, the truth, and the life" (John 14:6), and "I am the true vine" (John 15:1).

Did Rowling have this in mind when she had Harry identify himself to Ron and Hermione—"It's me"? Why did he need to say it at all unless she wanted to identify him with the risen Christ?

At this same place in *The Deathly Hallows*, Rowling provides another curious reference to the Gospel stories, writing that Harry owes Ron and Hermione an explanation of everything because they have "stuck with him for so long" and "deserved the truth." He talks to them as they walk along together. "Painstakingly he recounted what he had seen in the Pensieve and what had happened in the forest, and they had not even begun to express all their shock and amazement when at last they arrived at the place to which they had been walking, though none of them had mentioned their destination."[130]

Set beside that passage this one from the Gospel of Luke, which is after Jesus' resurrection:

Now on that same day two of them were going to a village called Emmaus, about seven miles from Jerusalem, and talking with each other about all these things that had happened. While they were talking and discussing, Jesus himself came near and went with them, but their eyes were kept from recognizing him. And he said to them, "What are you discussing with each other while you walk along?" They stood still, looking sad. Then one of them, whose name was Cleopas, answered him, "Are you the only stranger in Jerusalem who does not know the things that have taken place there in these days?" He asked them, "What things?" They replied, "The things about Jesus of Nazareth, who was a prophet mighty in deed and word before God and all the people, and how our chief priests and leaders handed him over to be condemned to death and crucified him. But we had hoped that he was the one to redeem Israel...." Then he said to them, "Oh, how foolish you are and how slow of heart to believe all that the prophets have declared. Was it not necessary that the Messiah should suffer these things and then enter into his glory?" Then beginning with Moses and all the prophets, he interpreted to them the things about himself in all the scriptures.

As they came near the village to which they were going, he walked ahead as if he were going on. But they urged him strongly, saying, "Stay with us, because it is almost evening and the day is now nearly over." So he went in to stay with them. When he was at the table with them, he took bread, blessed and broke it, and gave it to them. Then their eyes were opened, and they recognized him; and he vanished from their sight. (Luke 24:13–31)

Harry and his friends are walking somewhere, with him explaining as they go. Like these disciples of Jesus, Ron and Hermione are filled with "shock and amazement." Then, as Jesus and the two disciples do, they arrive at their destination. Are these connections mere coincidence?

Add one more. Harry, Ron, and Hermione's unspecified destination is Dumbledore's office. Harry, on entering, glimpses the stone Pensieve on Dumbledore's desk, and then "an earsplitting noise made him cry out, thinking of curses and returning Death Eaters and the rebirth of Voldemort." But it was the sound of great applause: "All around the walls, the headmasters and headmistresses of Hogwarts were giving him a standing ovation; they waved their hats and in some cases their wigs, they reached through their frames to grasp each other's hands; they danced up and down on the chairs in which they had been painted."[131] It is a wonderful moment and easily reminds us of the "loud voices in heaven" from the book of Revelation: "The kingdom of the world has become the kingdom of our Lord and of his Messiah, and he will reign forever and ever!" (Rev 11:15).

7

HAPPY EVER AFTERING

I imagine J. K. Rowling and her editors spent some time discussing the epilogue of her series, titled "Nineteen Years Later," and whether it actually belonged at the end of the seven-volume narrative or ought to be scrapped and left unsaid. Its tone is quite different from that of everything that comes before. It's a little like appearing at the breakfast table the morning after a fabulous, memorable party in one's dirty old shorts and flip-flops.

It is only seven pages long in the deluxe edition. The writing is clean and pictorial:

> Autumn seemed to arrive suddenly that year. The morning of the first of September was crisp and golden as an apple, and as the little family bobbed across the rumbling road toward the great sooty station, the fumes of car exhausts and the breath of pedestrians sparkled like cobwebs in the cold air. Two large cases rattled on top of the laden trolleys the parents were pushing; the owls inside them hooted indignantly, and the redheaded girl trailed tearfully behind her brothers, clutching her father's arm.[132]

We are quickly into the story, or *after*-story, in this case. The little redheaded girl is Lily, Harry and Ginny's daughter—named for his mother—and she cries because she wants to go to Hogwarts like her brothers, James and Albus. They push their trolleys through King's Cross Station, headed for the now-familiar secret passageway to platform 9 3/4.

On the platform they meet Ron and Hermione and their two children, Rose and Hugo, and also Draco Malfoy and his wife and boy Scorpius. When Ginny hugs James, she tells him to give their love to Professor Neville Longbottom. Harry reminds Albus that Hagrid has invited him to tea the following Friday, and warns him not to mess with Peeves, the irascible old poltergeist.

As the train departs from the station, the other students peer out the windows to see Harry. "Why are they all *staring*?" complains Albus. "Don't let it worry you," says Ron. "It's me. I'm extremely famous."[133] Harry feels something like "a little bereavement" at his son's departure for school. Ginny assures him he'll be all right. Harry touches his lightning scar and agrees that he will. "The scar had not pained Harry for nineteen years. All was well."[134]

Why *did* Rowling add this postscript to her books? What was she trying to convey?

One theory is that she wanted to assure her readers Voldemort is truly gone and no longer troubles Harry, Ron, Hermione, and the rest of the wizarding world. The fact that Harry's scar no longer bothers him is evidence of this.

Another is that she was simply extolling *ordinary* life—the kind of life most people live when they aren't at war or dealing with terrorism or great theological issues or anything else of enormous consequence. Harry and his friends are raising their children in a normal, peaceful society, facing everyday problems like nursing sick children, earning a living, cleaning the house, and deciding where to go on the family holiday.

At the figurative level—that is, with Harry as a Christ figure—Rowling may have been thinking of something else altogether. She may have been influenced, as I suggested earlier, by the extraordinary wave of interest stirred up by Dan Brown's novel *The Da Vinci Code*. Next to the Harry Potter books, *The Da Vinci Code* was probably the most popular and influential work of its decade. By 2006 it had sold more than 60 million copies worldwide and been translated into 44 languages, and it produced numerous clones and commentaries.

The Da Vinci Code is a mystery story, set mostly in France, about a secret that has been closely guarded until Jacques Saunière is found murdered in Paris. Saunière was Grand Master of the Priory of Sion and killed for the secret location of the "keystone" that led to the Holy Grail and certain documents guaranteed to shake the foundations of the Roman Catholic Church. The documents involved Leonardo da Vinci, also a member of the Priory of Sion, who left coded messages in his paintings about the information guarded by the Priory. The information concerned a marriage between Jesus and Mary Magdalene and their daughter named Sarah who was born after Jesus died and Mary Magdalene fled to Gaul, where Jews of Marseilles sheltered her. The bloodline of Jesus and Mary Magdalene, joined in their offspring, became the Merovingian dynasty of France.

Crusaders discovered this information after the fall of Jerusalem in 1099, and the Priory of Sion and the Knights Templar organization were formed to protect the secret. The Vatican feared that if the secret got out, it would undermine the papal authority and destroy the Roman Catholic Church.

According to certain theorists (Dan Brown was not the first or the last to be attracted to these historical rumors), Leonardo painted the secret into one of his most famous paintings, *The Last Supper*. Some people believe that the figure generally identified as the Apostle John, on Jesus' right, was actually Mary Magdalene, and the appellation "the disciple whom Jesus loved" refers to her, not to John. In the painting, she and Jesus wear corresponding colors, and she leans away from Jesus to the left while he leans to the right, forming a large V in the painting, which symbolizes the Sacred Feminine. According to the theory, the Holy Grail, which has eluded seekers for centuries, isn't a vessel at all, but rather Mary Magdalene. Thus, Leonardo omitted a chalice in his painting because he intended for viewers to understand Mary Magdalene herself as the sacred vessel, the one bearing Jesus' blood in her womb.

The Old French words for Holy Grail were *san gréal*, a play on *sang réal*, or "royal blood." Again, according to the theory, Mary Magdalene was descended from the House of David, and so was herself of royal blood and was the true *sang réal* or Holy Grail. Supposedly, the Roman Catholic Church created the story of her prostitution to denigrate the power of the feminine, which might otherwise have challenged the primacy of Simon Peter and the male line of papal descent.

How does this relate to the Harry Potter saga? It is speculative, of course, but nevertheless highly suggestive. J. K. Rowling doesn't offer more secrets in her brief final chapter, "Nineteen Years

Later"—she deals with plenty over the course of the novels—but she does use the brief chapter to show us her Christ figure, Harry, as a married man with children of his own. Perhaps it is the sort of happy-ever-after scenario we are left to imagine for Mary Magdalene and Sarah, Jesus' daughter, in *The Da Vinci Code* and other books that revolve around the search for the Holy Grail.

The same reasoning, if it can be called that, might also suggest why Harry and Hermione have such a close relationship in the novels. In *The Deathly Hallows*, when Ron gets angry with Harry in the forest and leaves, not reappearing for weeks, Hermione stays with Harry and accompanies him to Godric's Hollow. She isn't strictly a Mary Magdalene figure, for she and Harry never wed. But she does represent a female presence in the novels that is reminiscent of the recent revelations about Mary Magdalene and her adoration of Jesus.

The Gospel of Mary, part of the Nag Hammadi library recovered in the mid-twentieth century, offers a revealing passage in which the Apostle Peter says to Mary Magdalene, "Sister, we know that the Savior loved you more than the rest of women. Tell us the words of the Savior which you remember—which you remember but we do not, nor have we heard them." Mary Magdalene responds, "What is hidden from you I will proclaim to you," and she proceeds to instruct them in what she knows about Jesus—things they don't know.[135] Peter and Andrew, among the apostles, represented a prejudice in the early church against women leaders and teachers. But this so-called Gnostic gospel points to the possibility of a different conclusion than the one we generally reach about the position of women in the first-century church, and this, as much as anything, has fueled such astonishing interest in *The Da*

Vinci Code and other books that counter the patristic emphasis of the Roman Catholic Church through the centuries.

In a 2001 BBC interview, Rowling said she gave Hermione an unusual name so fewer girls would be teased about having the same name as the smart-mouthed, independent lass of the Harry Potter stories, and that Hermione's character was actually modeled largely on Rowling's own—quick, clever, studious, but often shunned in school because of these qualities. At some point, Rowling also indicated that she took the name from Hermione, Leontes's queen in Shakespeare's *The Winter's Tale*, who was also clever and outspoken for her time. The name is actually Greek in origin: *'er-may-o-ne*, which is almost certainly related to *'er-may-nay-a*, the root of our word "hermeneutic," which means "interpretation." This term certainly applies to Hermione in the Harry Potter stories, who, more than any other friends of Harry, is given to interpreting everything. It would also be in the character of Mary Magdalene, who told the male disciples about Jesus.

Was Rowling attempting to say more than meets the eye by making Hermione a disciple and close companion of Harry? Did she intend for astute readers to understand that Hermione somehow represented Mary Magdalene and all the women in Jesus' life who were obviously important in his ministry both before and after his death—news of the resurrection was conveyed first *to the women*—and to that extent at least rewrite early Christian history? We cannot, I think, put it past her, for she is indeed a cunning and clever writer, much like the young woman about whom she wrote.

The Number Nineteen

Why *nineteen* years? Why not twenty, or eighteen, or sixteen?

Rowling probably had her own reason for that—or none at all. Of course, she isn't required to have had one. She could have picked it out of a hat, though such methods are not typical for her.

Nineteen years elapsed between the Treaty of Versailles in 1919, which officially settled affairs in Europe after World War I, and Hitler's invasion of Austria and Sudetenland in 1938, which effectually initiated World War II. Maybe Rowling was reminding us of the sheer periodicity of evil in the world, the way it seems to ebb and flow through the centuries, like some vast cycle of the globe itself.

Harry is eleven when he first goes to Hogwarts and seventeen when he defeats Voldemort and life returns to normal. We assume he, Ron, and Hermione went back to Hogwarts for their final year of classes, which they missed during their search for the Horcruxes and the great apocalyptic battle at the end of the earlier school year. Thus, they would have all been eighteen years old at graduation. At the time of the epilogue, they would be thirty-six—relatively young witches and wizards at the height of their powers.

Perhaps nineteen was simply a good, nondescript number, one that we couldn't—and shouldn't—load with interpretations. After seven volumes of stories in which numerology often plays a part, Rowling may have wanted a number that signifies absolutely nothing to her readers. As nineteen is indivisible by any other number except one and itself, she obviously found such a number. It is totally unromantic and completely insignificant.

I am fascinated by the image of the school children hanging out the train windows to stare at Harry. Is it some kind of adoration—the kind human beings have always paid to saviors? Or is it tinged with irony, like the autograph seekers who clamored after Tom Selleck only to be disappointed when they learned he wasn't Clark Gable?

By the same token, the picture of Draco Malfoy and the way he is ill at ease with the others saddens me. That name, "Dragon Bad Faith," has been an awful burden to him. It must have had a terribly negative influence on his life. And to call his little son "Scorpius" is just as bad, maybe worse. I'm afraid the boy is fated to play the heavy, with a name like that. He will be a mean-spirited player on the Quidditch field, a bully in the locker room, and a snitch in the classroom. And I can't imagine any girl's father taking lightly to Scorpius's proposing to marry his daughter and make her "Mrs. Scorpion Bad Faith."

As long as Rowling imagined a pleasant ending for her often tumultuous and upsetting novels, why didn't she choose for Draco's son a name like Pax or Noble or something more palatable than Scorpius? Why didn't she depict Draco and his wife enjoying a pleasant conversation with the Potters and the Weasleys—even promising to get together for lunch at the next opportunity?

She is right, of course. Leopards seldom lose their spots, and amends between bitter enemies rarely last long before there's a new spat or conflict of some kind. Nobody promised us a rose garden. There will always be wars and rumors of wars, and there will always be a need for some new Harry Potter to come along and deal with the latest version of Lord Voldemort.

Maybe that's the reason for the raw, chafed creature that troubles us in Rowling's version of heaven, the one that is like the shriveled-up soul of the Dark Lord. Even heaven itself may not be entirely perfect.

Love Conquers All

Amor vincit omnia, reads the crowned inscription on the "broche of gold ful shene" worn by Eglentyne, the mild and smiling prioress of Chaucer's *Canterbury Tales*—"Love conquers all." In the end, this may be the message Rowling wishes us to understand from her epilogue: that love is eventually victorious in everything, though it isn't always the glorious, passionate love glamorized by soap operas and romance novels. Instead, it is often the simple, sometimes less than demonstrative love of husbands and wives and families going about the ordinary pleasures and duties of their lives, as exemplified in embracing and admonishing their children before sending them off to boarding school.

After all, Lily's love for her baby Harry saved him from Voldemort's killing curse. Harry always knew his mother gave her life for his. His father, too, shouted to Lily to run, to take the child and escape, but it was too late. Harry sees his parents again in the first novel, *The Sorcerer's Stone*, through the Mirror of Erised—"desire" spelled backward. Standing alone before the mirror, eleven-year-old Harry sees himself, "white and scared-looking." Then he sees a woman smiling and waving. "She was a very pretty woman. She had dark red hair and her eyes—*her eyes are just like mine*, Harry thought, edging a little closer to the glass. Bright green—exactly the same shape, but then he noticed that she was crying; smiling, but crying at the same time. The tall, thin, black-haired man standing next to her put his arm around her. He wore glasses, and his hair was very untidy. It stuck up at the back, just as Harry's did."[136]

His parents appear at the end of the story, too, in *The Deathly Hallows*, coming to him with Sirius Black and Remus Lupin in the woods between death and life. In the epilogue, two of Harry and Ginny's children bear their names: James and Lily. Through the course of the novels, there is never a time when Harry's parents are absent.

Rowling is convinced of the power and importance of love. She sets a quotation from William Penn, founder of the Friends movement or Quaker sect, at the head of her final novel: "Death is but crossing the world, as friends do the seas; they live in one another still. For they must needs be present, that love and live in that which is omnipresent. In this divine glass, they see face to face; and their converse is free, as well as pure. This is the comfort of friends, that though they may be said to die, yet their friendship and society are, in the best sense, ever present, because immortal." This beautiful saying defines the boundaries of the narrative. Not even death is able to separate friends and loved ones. Voldemort seeks power, but is vanquished in the end by one who loves deeply and cares nothing for earthly dominion. Dumbledore tells Harry in *The Order of the Phoenix*, when the boy grieves for his godfather Sirius Black, "There is no shame in what you are feeling, Harry. On the contrary…the fact that you can feel pain like this is your greatest strength."[137] In his anguish, Harry finally blurts out, "I don't care! I've had enough, I've seen enough, I want out, I want it to end, I don't care anymore—" "You do care," says Dumbledore.

"You care so much you feel as though you will bleed to death with the pain of it."[138]

Dumbledore can talk this way because he too cares about people. Lord Voldemort taunts him, in *The Half-Blood Prince*, "Nothing I have seen in the world has supported your famous pronouncements that love is more powerful than my kind of magic." "Perhaps," says Dumbledore, "you have been looking in the wrong places."[139]

Later, talking with Harry, Dumbledore observes that it will take "uncommon skill and power" to kill a wizard like Voldemort. Harry protests that he doesn't possess such skill and power. Dumbledore insists that he does: he has *the power to love*. "So," asks Harry, "when the prophecy says that I'll have 'power the Dark Lord knows not,' it just means—love?" "Yes," Dumbledore responds, "just love."[140]

Nothing we know about Dumbledore—not his supposed omniscience, not the fact that he is "the greatest wizard Harry had ever, or would ever, meet,"[141] not his wisdom as a schoolmaster, not his uncanny skill at reading people—bespeaks his likeness to God the Father more than his tireless ability to keep loving even when others betray his faith in them. He loves Harry and his friends. He loves Severus Snape and trusts him even when others are certain he is spying for Voldemort. After Dumbledore dies, when Remus Lupin resists Tonks's affection for him, Professor McGonagall says, "Dumbledore would have been happier than anybody to think that there was a little more love in the world."[142]

As she wrote the Potter books, Rowling met and married a new husband. Undoubtedly, this is one reason she adds the "Nineteen Years Later" epilogue: the love of two people for each other that leads to marriage and family is as important to her as Dumbledore's early love for Grindelwald and his love for Harry Potter.

The subject of love is important in one other way in the Harry Potter literature, and that is with respect to the love Harry and Hermione and other witches and wizards have for Muggles, house-elves, centaurs, and the rest of those unlike themselves. Dumbledore, who as a young man was angry with the Muggles who attacked his little sister, gains quite another reputation as he grows older. Harry, Hermione, and Ron overhear Draco Malfoy on the Hogwarts Express talking about how his father almost sent him to Durmstrang for school instead of Hogwarts because of his opinion of Dumbledore—"the man's such a Mudblood-lover."[143] "Mudbloods" is a derogatory term for witches or wizards of non-pureblood parentage.

Hermione becomes a veritable crusader for the rights of house-elves, the indentured servants who perform many of the menial tasks in wizard homes. When a house-elf called Winky is falsely accused of using Harry's wand to produce the Death Mark over the Quidditch World Cup match in *The Goblet of Fire*, Hermione asks Arthur Weasley what will happen to her. He says he doesn't know, angering Hermione. "The way they were treating her! …Mr. Diggory, calling her 'elf' all the time…and Mr. Crouch! He knows she didn't do it and he's still going to sack her! He didn't care how frightened she'd been, or how upset she was—it was like she wasn't even human!"[144] Americans familiar with the racial problems of the United States will recognize Hermione's indignation.

During the self-styled "Elf Liberation Movement" led by Hermione, Dumbledore gives Winky refuge at Hogwarts, along with Dobby and more than a hundred other house-elves. Dobby explains to Harry that he has looked for work for two years but can't find any that pays a wage for services performed until Dumbledore takes them in, giving them tea towels embroidered with the Hogwarts crest, which the elves use as togas to outfit themselves.

The elves like working for Dumbledore: "Professor Dumbledore offered Dobby ten Galleons a week, and weekends off," the house-elf explains to Hermione, "but Dobby beat him down, miss.... Dobby likes freedom, miss, but he isn't wanting too much, miss, he likes work better."[145] Harry and the elves get along famously: he and Dobby even exchange Christmas presents. And Hermione is pleased that Dumbledore gives the elves work, because she believes it will encourage other house-elves to seek paid work. However, even as some wizards and witches befriend the house-elves, others begin campaigning to restrict all creatures who are not pureblood.

The final volume of the series, *The Deathly Hallows,* opens with a horrifying scene: Voldemort, his snake Nagini, and his Death Eater friends are gathered in a Muggle house they have commandeered and are discussing matters around a slowly revolving body suspended above them. It is a teacher from Hogwarts named Charity Burbage, who has been charged with "corrupting and polluting the minds of Wizarding children" by writing an impassioned defense of Mudbloods in the *Daily Prophet,* contending that the world would be better with fewer purebloods. From time to time, Voldemort flicks Burbage with his wand, causing her spasms of pain. At the end of the meeting, he kills her with the *Avada Kedavra* curse.

As the final showdown between the Dark Lord's people and Dumbledore's Army approaches, the Death Eaters increase their persecution. Dolores Umbridge is appointed Head of the Muggle-born Registration Commission for the Ministry of Magic, and the ministry sets about gathering Mudbloods, Muggles, centaurs, rebellious house-elves, and anyone else who doesn't conform to Voldemort's standards of genetic purity. Umbridge calls centaurs "filthy half-breeds." Gangs of Snatchers roam the countryside like Nazi patrols, rounding up anyone suspected of a mixed background. Hermione's parents, who are Muggles (non-magical people), flee to Australia.

Hermione, Harry, and Ron roam the countryside like criminals in hiding. There is a high price on Harry's head, and everybody is looking for him. Rowling's prose is, as usual, spare and highly descriptive: "Autumn rolled over the countryside as they moved through it: They were now pitching the tent on mulches of fallen leaves. Natural mists joined those cast by the dementors; wind and rain added to their troubles. The fact that Hermione was getting better at identifying edible fungi could not altogether compensate for their continuing isolation, the lack of other people's company, or their total ignorance of what was going on in the war against Voldemort."[146]

A side note to our subject here is worth noting. One night, as the three friends eat supper, Ron prods at the "lumps of charred gray fish on his plate" and reminisces about the way his mother can "make good food appear out of thin air." Hermione corrects him, noting that food is one of the five "Principal Exceptions to Gamp's

Law of Elemental Transfiguration." Essentially, one can magically move food from one place to another, but one cannot simply create it "out of thin air."[147]

This exchange could be an oblique reference to the passages in the Gospels that refer to Jesus' feeding multitudes of people on a few fishes and loaves of bread (Matt 14:13–21; 15:32–39; Mark 6:30–44; 8:1–10; Luke 9:10–17; John 6:1–14). Jesus' miracle has often been the subject of debates within Christian circles concerning whether the feedings were actual or symbolic; the feedings are often cited as having some relationship to the ritual of the Lord's Supper or Eucharist.

The wizarding world, in *The Half-Blood Prince* and *The Deathly Hallows*, increasingly forms into two distinctly different camps: those who love all kinds of creatures and accept their natural differences, and those who hate and fear others and are intolerant of differences. Rowling skillfully introduces touches that enable her readers to identify the behavior of the Ministry of Magic with various oppressive movements in not-so-distant world history: the international slave trade, fascism, Nazism, racial profiling, gender discrimination, prejudicial hiring, and in fact any kind of modern racism.

Harry, Ron, and Hermione listen to the contraband wireless broadcast of a program called *Potterwatch,* whose signal is frequently changed to evade a shutdown by the ministry, and they hear a news report about five members of a Muggle family found dead in their home. The reporter continues, "Muggle authorities are attributing the deaths to a gas leak, but members of the Order of the Phoenix inform me that it was the Killing Curse—more evidence, as if it were needed, of the fact that Muggle slaughter is becoming little more than a recreational sport under the new regime."[148] Ironically, one of the creatures many wizards disdain—the long-persecuted house-elves—comes to the aid of Harry Potter and his friends when Bellatrix Lestrange and Narcissa Malfoy hold them captive, waiting for Voldemort to arrive and kill Harry. The elf Dobby, who once worked for Narcissa but is freed and has developed a strong friendship with Harry, suddenly appears in their midst and orders Narcissa not to hurt Harry Potter. When Bellatrix accuses him of defying his masters, Dobby declares, "Dobby has no master! ...Dobby is a free elf, and Dobby has come to save Harry Potter and his friends!"[149]

Dobby's quest succeeds, but it costs him his life. Harry, out of his great humanitarian respect, insists on burying Dobby the old-fashioned way—by actually digging his grave with spades instead of simply creating it with a wand. When the hole is deep enough, Harry wraps the little body in his jacket. Ron removes his socks and puts them on the tiny feet. Someone else produces a woolen hat, which Harry places on Dobby's head. They all stand reverently around the grave, thanking Dobby for rescuing them and for being "so good and brave." Harry places a stone from the sea at the head of the grave. Then, drawing out his wand and murmuring instructions, he engraves the stone with these words: "Here lies Dobby, a free elf." [150]

This scene is the epitome of love in the Harry Potter books—love for a simple little house-elf, love for the smallest, most insignificant creature around them, love for "the very least of these," as the Christian gospel puts it. In a sense, it sums up everything Rowling was trying to say in all the books, in the thousands of pages of them: in the end, *love* counts, not power.

The commitment of people to one another in genuine caring and fidelity is essential; the sense of unity that grows out of a fondness for life itself, for creation, for the way things are made and fit together, and especially for other people who travel this way with us is beyond comparison.

Professor Quirrell, the Dark Lord's servant who carries Voldemort around enswathed in his own turban, says in *The Sorcerer's Stone*, "There is no good and evil, there is only power, and those too weak to seek it."[151] There is even a time when Dumbledore, like the God of the Old Testament, seems to agree about the importance of power. But in the end, Dumbledore sides with love, like the God of the New Testament, and praises Harry Potter because Harry has a loving heart that not even death can still.

Death, as Rowling demonstrates, has no control or power over love, for love endures beyond the grave. This is why Dumbledore can say, "After all, to the well-organized mind, death is but the next great adventure,"[152] and why Harry can declare, after Dumbledore dies, that his beloved headmaster will be gone "only when none here are loyal to him."[153] It is also why, when Harry defeats Voldemort, there is such universal applause for what he has done—from the centaurs, the giants, the house-elves, even the ghosts of former headmasters and headmistresses in their portrait frames.

It is the consummation of which St. Paul dreams in his letter to the Romans, the redemption of all creation, which has in Christ been "set free from its bondage to decay" to "obtain the freedom of the glory of the children of God" (Rom 8:21). Harry Potter, in Rowling's long and rambling analogue on the gospel story, is the one who brings about redemption!

Is Harry a Christ figure? Without a doubt. Is Dumbledore God the Father? Probably, though at times an unlikely one. Is J. K. Rowling consciously mimicking the pattern of the gospel stories in her novels about Harry? Again, I believe it is without a doubt.

Does this in any way impugn Rowling's gifts as a literary artist? Not in the least. In fact, it is a tribute to her extraordinary imagination that she was able to disguise her dependence on the gospel stories so cleverly that almost no one guessed her intentions until the publication of the final novel, in which she more generously and dramatically reveals her fealty to "the greatest story ever told." Owing to her exceptional creativity, the Harry Potter stories can stand well on their own without overt reference to the life and ministry of Christ; but also owing to that creativity, the Potter saga now exists as a fine embellishment on the Christian gospel.

Consider, in the final analysis, the "clues" Rowling provides in her series that permit us to reach the conclusions stated in this book:

(1) Lord Voldemort attempts to murder the infant Harry, whose very existence threatens him, as Herod attempted to murder baby Jesus.

(2) The lightning-shaped scar on Harry's forehead may be related to the God who confronted Moses at the burning bush. Some scholars believe the name God gave Moses, "I am who I am," was originally the word for a bolt of lightning.

(3) The strange happenings surrounding the delivery of the infant Harry to his aunt and uncle's house—numerous wizard sightings, shooting stars, numerous owls flying in the daytime, the tall wizard who snuffs out streetlamps, a witch disguised as a cat—

remind us of the unusual occurrences at the birth of Jesus: extraordinary prophecies, angels speaking to shepherds, and magi (second-tier magicians) following an unusually brilliant star to see the child.

(4) Harry's conspicuous involvement in acts of magic parallel Jesus' reputation as a master magician and healer. Miraculous occurrences are attached to both their childhoods. The *Gospel of Thomas* records Jesus' bringing a salted fish back to life, and the apocryphal book of James tells that when he was five and reprimanded by Joseph for playing with clay birds he had formed, he simply made them fly away. In Harry's case, his hair grows back overnight after his Aunt Petunia cuts off most of it; a revolting sweater Aunt Petunia makes for him becomes so small he can't get it over his head; and once, when Dudley and his bully friends chase Harry, he tries to leap over garbage cans and finds himself sitting atop a chimney over the school kitchen. And, of course, the rest of Jesus' and Harry's lives were deeply involved in magical/miraculous acts.

(5) Harry's ability to understand and speak Parseltongue— even though he is not of the House of Slytherin—and Voldemort's getting into his mind by Legilimency suggest that he has a dual nature like Christ's, who was believed to be both human and divine.

(6) Dumbledore's insistence that Harry's suffering proves he is "still a man"—"This pain," he says, "is part of being human"[154]—is like the Gospels' frequent reminder that Jesus is a human being, albeit a special one.

(7) Voldemort's playing with Harry's mind may be seen as related to the devil's temptations of Jesus in the wilderness, when

the devil offered him power, wisdom, and acclamation if Jesus would fall down and worship him.

(8) Harry's close relationship with his friends or disciples, specifically Ron, Hermione, and Neville, and the fact that he actually teaches them and other students Defense Against the Dark Arts, is similar to the friendship of Jesus with his disciples Peter, James, and John, whom he constantly taught the secrets of the kingdom.

(9) Harry's role as Seeker on the Quidditch team, and his ability to fly faster than others and spot and seize the Golden Snitch, may represent Jesus' role as seeker of the divine and his unusual ability to capture the truth and express it in unforgettable ways.

(10) Harry's use of the Invisibility Cloak to visit people and places unobserved reminds us of Jesus' mysterious way of coming and going in the Gospels, even, after the resurrection, appearing suddenly through bolted doors.

(11) Harry's willingness throughout the novels to sacrifice himself for others who are in danger, and, in the end, to give his life to save them, is extraordinarily Christlike. In *The Chamber of Secrets*, Dobby says, "Harry Potter risks his own life for his friends."[155]

(12) Harry's expressed desire to become an Auror after graduation from Hogwarts—a Ministry of Magic worker who has scored exceptionally high levels on his exams and successfully completed "a stringent series of character and aptitude tests"—is roughly equivalent to Jesus' becoming a rabbi in the Jewish religious tradition. Dolores Umbridge, who works for the ministry,

scoffs at Harry's ability to qualify for such a post, just as many scribes and Pharisees disputed Jesus' authority as a teacher.

(13) The assurance that Harry is really his father's son (Sirius Black tells him, "You are—truly your father's son, Harry"[156]) reminds us of the controversy over whether Jesus was actually the son of his heavenly Father, as he often claimed to be, especially in the Fourth Gospel.

(14) Dumbledore's phoenix Fawkes rescues Harry from impossible situations in the same way that Jesus was rescued by the Holy Spirit, and comes to him in an emergency because he is being loyal to Dumbledore.

(15) Harry has the same humble, self-effacing nature ("so modest," Professor Slughorn says[157]) as Christ, whom St. Paul describes in Philippians 2 as "emptying himself" for our salvation and assuming the role of a slave.

(16) Like Jesus, Harry has a growing awareness of his mission and shows a stubborn commitment to it, regardless of the cost. "I always knew I'd have to face [Voldemort] in the end," he says in *The Half-Blood Prince*.[158] Later, he asserts, "I am the chosen one. I have to kill him."[159]

(17) Harry, again like Jesus, displays a healthy disregard for rules and regulations that thwart or interfere with one's duty to others. Jesus was often accused of breaking cleansing laws or Sabbath injunctions for the sake of others.

(18) Hermione tells Harry that he has "a saving-people-thing"—certainly a reference to Jesus' mission as Savior of the world.[160]

(19) Harry's real power over Voldemort is his ability to love—an ability Voldemort doesn't have—in the same way that Jesus

stood for the love of God and taught his disciples to love in spite of the way the world treated them. Most notably, Jesus forgave his own crucifiers from the cross.

(20) Harry, Ron, and Hermione, vilified by the press and the Ministry of Magic, live as outcasts in the wilderness, as Jesus and his disciples apparently did at times. Harry, like Jesus during the final days of his ministry, is "the most wanted person in the country" and is talked about everywhere.[161]

(21) Harry undergoes a kind of baptism to get the sword of Gryffindor from the pool in the forest, just as Jesus accepted baptism from the prophet John the Baptist in the River Jordan.

(22) Aberforth Dumbledore, Albus's brother, warns Harry to "go abroad, go into hiding, save yourself"[162]—surely one of the temptations of Jesus in his last days—but like Jesus Harry denies himself in order to save others.

(23) Ron defects from Harry when they are under pressure, just as Simon Peter denied Jesus before his crucifixion, and Ron apologizes and asks Harry's forgiveness, just as Peter confessed and was forgiven.

(24) The reference in *The Deathly Hallows* to increasing the amount of food by magic—while Harry, Ron, and Hermione are eating *fish!*—is reminiscent of the feeding miracles in the wilderness, when Jesus multiplied the loaves and fishes the disciples brought him and thereby fed great multitudes of people.

(25) Harry takes the part of the house-elves, centaurs, Muggles, Mudbloods, and other creatures of low status against the self-righteous purebloods in the Ministry of Magic, as Jesus in his time took the part of the poor, sick, and religiously outcast against the scribes and Pharisees.

(26) The expectation among Harry's friends, expressed by Luna Lovegood, that if he came back "it would mean revolution,"[163] is exactly the same as that among Jesus' followers, who thought his appearance in Jerusalem would produce an upheaval and introduce the reign of God.

(27) The scene on Christmas Eve in Godric's Hollow, when the war memorial changes into a statue of James, Lily, and Harry, is precisely the scene we always identify with Christmas Eve, that of the Holy Family in the stable.

(28) Harry feels abandoned by Dumbledore and complains that his headmaster has introduced him to his mission but not shown him how to accomplish it, in the same way that Jesus cried out from the cross, "My God, my God, why have you forsaken me?" (Matt 27:46).

(29) There is an emphasis on Harry's shedding of blood, just as there was on Jesus' shedding his blood. In *The Goblet of Fire*, Wormtail takes some of Harry's blood to help revive Voldemort, and in *The Half-Blood Prince*, Dumbledore tells Harry, "Your blood is worth more than mine."[164] The Gospel writers and subsequent Christian authors all spoke with great reverence of Jesus' blood as being the perfect sacrifice for sin.

(30) The image of the heart-shaped locket that burns into Harry's flesh in *The Deathly Hallows* is suggestive of the popular image of the Sacred Heart in medieval and modern devotionalism, particularly in the literature and iconography of the Society of Jesus.

(31) Harry's vision in *The Deathly Hallows* of "an object that looked like a skull, and something like a mountain,"[165] is suggestive

of Golgotha, the place of the skull, where Jesus was crucified outside the city of Jerusalem.

(32) Dolores Umbridge's use of the *Cruciatus* curse to force people to talk and give up one another during the Ministry of Magic's purge could be a reference to the way the Romans employed crucifixion as a means of threatening Christians during the years of their persecution following the death of Jesus.

(33) Harry's eventually submitting to Dumbledore's suggestion that he leave the safety of their heavenly vale and return to battle Voldemort again is a reminder of the way Jesus submitted to God's leadership in the Garden of Gethsemane, praying, "Not my will, but your will be done" (Mark 14:36).

(34) Voldemort strikes Harry with the *Cruciatus* curse—an obvious reference to the crucifixion of Jesus—and tosses his body into the air with the kind of pain and distress we naturally associate with the agony of Jesus on the cross.

(35) Harry lies in a coma for three days after his battle with the great basilisk in the Chamber of Secrets—the exact duration of the time Jesus lay in the tomb after his crucifixion.

(36) Harry's descent into the Chamber of Secrets, where he battles the basilisk to rescue Ginny Weasley, is reminiscent of the popular legend of Jesus' Descent into Hell to rescue the souls imprisoned there by the devil.

(37) The dead come back to walk with Harry when he returns to meet Voldemort again, reminding us of the phenomenon mentioned in Matthew 27:52–53 when the tombs in Jerusalem were opened during Jesus' hours on the cross and "many bodies of the saints who had fallen asleep were raised" and, following the

resurrection, "came out of the tombs and entered the holy city and appeared to many."

(38) Voldemort tells everyone that Harry was killed while trying to save himself, recalling the taunting of Jesus by his enemies around the cross, who said, "He saved others; let him save himself if he is the Messiah of God, his chosen one!" (Luke 23:35; note the phrase "*the chosen one*").

(39) Harry returns from death—which Rowling depicts as peaceful and pleasant—to deal Voldemort his final defeat, just as Jesus came back from the grave to visit his disciples and inspire them to organize the church and continue to resist the powers of evil and death. Furthermore, it is Easter Day when this occurs, and Harry's followers scream "He's alive!" from every side, just as millions of Christians around the world still greet the morning of Easter Day with the cry, "He is risen! Hallelujah, he is alive forevermore!"

(40) Harry says, "It's me," to Ron and Hermione after his return, just as Jesus says, "It is I," to his disciples in his post-resurrection appearance to them in Mark 6:50 ("Take heart, it is I; do not be afraid") and the Jesus of the Fourth Gospel employs "It is I" (*ego eimi*) repeatedly as a sign of his resurrection presence.

(41) Harry walks with Ron and Hermione to explain to them all the things that have happened, just as Jesus walked with the disciples from Emmaus and taught them from the Scriptures about all that had taken place in Jerusalem when he was crucified.

(42) There is a biblical air of apocalypticism in the final battle at Hogwarts and Harry's victory over Voldemort and the Death Eaters, echoing the triumphalism of the early church, as in this passage from Revelation 14:1–5: "Then I looked, and there was the

mb, standing on Mount Zion! And with him were one hundred

'r thousand who had his name and his Father's name

'eir foreheads. And I heard a voice from heaven like

the   nany waters and like the sound of loud thunder; the

voice I heard was like the sound of harpists playing on their harps, and they sing a new song before the throne and before the four living creatures and before the elders.... They have been redeemed from humankind as first fruits for God and the Lamb, and in their mouth no lie was found; they are blameless."

(43) The whole atmosphere of Hogwarts after Harry's victory over Voldemort is one of love and celebration, just as the atmosphere of the church is supposed to be one of love and celebration, as ritualized in the Communion or Love Feast of believers, when grudges are forgiven, Christ's presence is emphasized, and, ideally, love reigns in everyone's heart.

There are undoubtedly many other similarities between Harry's story and Jesus'. Doctoral students gleaning information for their dissertations will doubtless discover them for years to come.

The amazing thing is how thoroughly Rowling has salted her story with these clues. She doesn't provide them in the order of their appearance in the Gospels, but (as I pointed out earlier) not even the Gospels themselves observe a strict order in their narratives about Jesus. Biblical scholars posit prior sources for the four written Gospels—proto-Mark, Q (from the German word *Quelle*, or source), a "sayings" source, and possibly others—and assume that the authors merely selected materials from those sources to suit their needs for particular kinds of material and inserted them into their narratives with no great respect for biographical order.

There are still depths to be plumbed: the meaning of Dumbledore and Harry's fateful trip across the strange underground sea in search of Bathilda Bagshot's locket, which unknown to them had been replaced by a fake; the late introduction of Aberforth Dumbledore into the narrative, and Harry's mistaking his eye in the shard of broken mirror for Albus Dumbledore's; the mysterious figure of Gellert Grindelwald, Dumbledore's friend in adolescence, who seems somehow unnecessary to the general narrative; the curious role of Severus Snape, who is Dumbledore's double agent with Voldemort; Draco Malfoy's hesitance to kill Dumbledore when he has the opportunity, and his "conversion" into a far milder, less diabolical person than we are led to believe he is; Luna Lovegood's role in the narrative (is *she* the Mary Magdalene of Rowling's story?); the deeper aspects of Rowling's cynicism about the press (e.g., Rita Skeeter's reporting style) and official bureaucracy; and perhaps the greater significance of the seven Horcruxes and three Deathly Hallows.

The Rowling corpus is already a goldmine of exploratory material for scholars and would-be scholars, and we haven't an inkling of what she will do next, now that she has acquitted herself of this Herculean task. That's without considering the amount of psychobabble that will be written about the author herself—single mother scribbling away in the corner of a café, living on the dole, managing to stay a step ahead of bill collectors, and fabricating this enormous *oeuvre* out of bits and pieces of ancient myths and legends, local superstitions, horror films, cartoons, esoteric formulas, necromancy manuals, jokes and splashes of humor, imaginative hogwash, and, woven in and out of it all, the central story of biblical faith. Rowling herself is great copy, and the press has loved her.

As I said in the dedication of this book, I fully expect that one day the world will regard J. K. Rowling with Dante, Shakespeare, and Dickens—from each of whom she has liberally borrowed—as part of the greatest quaternity of writers in the history of the world. If this expectation seems extravagant, well, remember that both Shakespeare and Dickens were considered hacks in their own time.

NOTES

[1] J. K. Rowling, *Harry Potter and the Deathly Hallows* (New York: Arthur A. Levine Books, 2007) 324.

[2] John Killinger, *God, the Devil, and Harry Potter* (New York: St. Martin's Press, 2002) 17–18.

[3] Richard Abanes, *Harry Potter and the Bible* (Camp Hill PA: Horizon Books, 2001) 97.

[4] Maria Tatar, quoted in Craig Lambert, "The Horror and the Beauty," *Harvard Magazine* 110/2 (Nov.–Dec. 2007): 41.

[5] J. K. Rowling, *Harry Potter and the Sorcerer's Stone* (New York: Arthur A. Levine Books, 1997) 10.

[6] Reported on *Newsweek's* web cast for 16 October 2007.

[7] Rowling, *Deathly Hallows,* 716.

[8] John Milton, *Paradise Lost,* book 1, lines 44–53.

[9] J. K. Rowling, *Harry Potter and the Half-Blood Prince* (New York: Arthur A. Levine Books, 2005) 642.

[10] Ibid., 643.

[11] Ibid., 645–46.

[12] Ibid., 645.

[13] Ibid., 646.

[14] Ibid., 648.

[15] Tatar quoted in Lambert, "The Horror and the Beauty," 41.

[16] Rowling, *Half-Blood Prince,* 177.

[17] Ibid., 498.

[18] J. K. Rowling, *Harry Potter and the Chamber of Secrets* (New York: Arthur A. Levine Books, 1998) 314.

[19] Ibid.

[20] Ibid., 315–25.

[21] Ibid., 332.

[22] Rowling, *Half-Blood Prince*, 645.

[23] Rowling, *Deathly Hallows*, 417.

[24] Killinger, *God, the Devil, and Harry Potter*, 62.

[25] Ibid., 64.

[26] J. K. Rowling, *Harry Potter and the Prisoner of Azkaban* (New York: Arthur A. Levine Books, 1999) 187.

[27] Ibid., 97.

[28] J. K. Rowling, *Harry Potter and the Order of the Phoenix* (New York: Arthur A. Levine Books, 2003) chap. 18, "Dumbledore's Army."

[29] Perhaps there is some connection between the name "Dumbledore's Army" and the often-used Christian appellation "the Army of the Lord." There may also be a hint of humor in the name if one recalls *Dad's Army*, a British TV comedy about the Home Guard during World War II, and how inept that ragtag group of misfits was for dealing with actual emergencies.

[30] Morton Smith, *Jesus the Magician: Charlatan or Son of God?* (Berkeley CA: Seastone/Ulysses Press, 1998).

[31] Rowling, *Order of the Phoenix*, 733.

[32] Ibid., 941.

[33] Rowling, *Half-Blood Prince*, 651.

[34] Rowling, *Deathly Hallows*, 273.

[35] Ibid., 372.

[36] Ibid., 391.

[37] Ibid., 730.

[38] Ibid., 731.

[39] Rowling, *Prisoner of Azkaban*, 324.

[40] J. K. Rowling, *Harry Potter and the Goblet of Fire* (New York, Arthur A. Levine Books, 2000) 129.

[41] Ibid., 640.

[42] Ibid., 643.

[43] Ibid., 646.

[44] Ibid., 657–58.

[45] Ibid., 653.

[46] Anne Lamott, *Plan B: Further Thoughts on Faith* (New York: Riverhead Books, 2006) 141–42.

[47] Rowling, *The Deathly Hallows*, 606.

[48] Rowling, *Half-Blood Prince*, 346.

[49] Rowling, *Goblet of Fire*, 733.

[50] Elton Trueblood, *The Humor of Christ* (New York: Harper and Row, 1964).

[51] Rowling, *Order of the Phoenix*, 603.

[52] Rowling, *Deathly Hallows*, 756.

[53] See my book *The Changing Shape of Our Salvation* (New York: Crossroad Publishing Co., 2007).

[54] That is, Matthew, Mark, and Luke. John, the Fourth Gospel, is another matter.

[55] Jaroslav Pelikan, *Jesus through the Centuries: His Place in the History of Culture* (New Haven: Yale University Press, 1985) 65.

[56] Rowling, *Sorcerer's Stone,* 176.

[57] Ibid., 270.

[58] Ibid., 283.

[59] Ibid., 293.

[60] Ibid., 295–96.

[61] Rowling, *Chamber of Secrets*, 16.

[62] Ibid., 179.

[63] Ibid., 194.

[64] Ibid., 501–502.

[65] Rowling, *Deathly Hallows*, 686.

[66] Mark 16:9; Luke 8:2.

[67] Ibid., 346.

[68] Rowling, *Deathly Hallows*, 699–701.

[69] Ibid., 705–706.

[70] Ibid., 707.

[71] Ibid., 726–27.

[72] Ibid., 436.

[73] T. S. Eliot, *Murder in the Cathedral,* in *The Complete Poems and Plays, 1909–1950* (New York: Harcourt, Brace, and Co., 1952) 194.

[74] 26 July 2007.

[75] Rowling, *Deathly Hallows*, 698–99.

[76] Killinger, *God, the Devil, and Harry Potter* , 129.

[77] Rowling, *Sorcerer's Stone*, 115.

[78] Rowling, *Chamber of Secrets*, chap. 8, "The Deathday Party."

[79] Rowling, *Deathly Hallows*, 701.

[80] For a summary of this tale, see the section "Another Set of Mysteries" in chapter 4 above.

[81] Rowling, *Deathly Hallows*, 328.

[82] Rowling, *Half-Blood Prince*, 445.

[83] Rowling, *Sorcerer's Stone*, 298.

[84] For more about Quirrell, see the section, "Harry's Proneness to Self-sacrifice," in chapter 4 above.

[85] Rowling, *Sorcerer's Stone*, 299.

[86] Ibid., 300.

[87] See chap. 21, "Hermione's Secret," in Rowling, *Prisoner of Azkaban.*.

[88] Rowling, *Goblet of Fire*, 722.

[89] Ibid., 724.

[90] Rowling, *Order of the Phoenix*, 826.

[91] Ibid., 838.

[92] Rowling, *Half-Blood Prince*, 197.

[93] Ibid., 508–509.

[94] Ibid., 509–11, my italics.

[95] Rowling, *Half-Blood Prince*, 570.

[96] Ibid., 578.

[97] Ibid., 585.

[98] Ibid., 596.

[99] Rowling, *Deathly Hallows*, 715–16.

[100] Ibid., 716.

[101] Ibid., 718.

[102] Ibid., 351.

[103] Ibid., 362.

[104] Ibid., 720–21.

[105] 26 July 2007.

[106] Rowling, *Deathly Hallows*, 654.

[107] Ibid., 691.

[108] Ibid., 707–708.

[109] Ibid.

[110] Rowling, *Goblet of Fire*, 642.

[111] Rowling, *Deathly Hallows*, 709.

[112] Ibid., 706–707.

[113] Ibid., 709.

[114] Ibid., 722.

[115] Rowling, *Goblet of Fire*, 640, my italics.

[116] Rowling, *Deathly Hallows*, 722.

[117] Ibid., 722–23.

[118] Jean-Paul Sartre, *Saint Gênet*, cited in introduction to Gênet's *The Maids*, trans. Bernard Frechtman (New York: Grove Press, 1954) 29.

[119] Ibid., 723.

[120] G. B. Shaw, *Saint Joan* (New York: Penguin Books, 1962) 59.

[121] Rowling, *Deathly Hallows*, 728.

[122] Ibid., 731.

[123] Ibid., 733–34.

[124] Ibid., 739.

[125] Ibid., 744.

[126] Ibid.

[127] Ibid., my italics.

[128] Rowling, *Deathly Hallows*, 745.

[129] Ibid., 746.

[130] Ibid.

[131] Ibid., 747.

[132] Rowling, *Deathly Hallows*, 753.

[133] Ibid., 759.

[134] Ibid.

[135] James M. Robinson, ed., *The Nag Hammadi Library in English* (San Francisco: Harper & Row, 1988) 525.

[136] Rowling, *Sorcerer's Stone*, 208.

137 Rowling, *Order of the Phoenix* , 823.

138 Ibid., 824.

139 Rowling, *Half-Blood Prince*, 444.

140 Ibid., 509.

141 Ibid., 608.

142 Ibid., 624.

143 Rowling, *Goblet of Fire*, 165.

144 Ibid., 139.

145 Ibid., 379.

146 Rowling, *Deathly Hallows*, 292.

147 Ibid., 292–93.

148 Ibid., 439.

149 Ibid., 474.

150 Ibid., 480–81.

151 Rowling, *Sorcerer's Stone*, 291.

152 Ibid., 297.

153 Rowling, *Half-Blood Prince*, 649.

154 Rowling, *Order of the Phoenix*, 824.

155 Rowling, *Chamber of Secrets*, 179.

156 Rowling, *Prisoner of Azkaban*, 415.

157 Rowling, *Half-Blood Prince*, 146.

158 Ibid., 98.

159 Ibid., 490.

160 Rowling, *Order of the Phoenix*, 733.

161 Rowling, *Deathly Hallows*, 210.

162 Ibid., 562.

163 Ibid., 581.

164 Rowling, *Half-Blood Prince*, 500.

165 Rowling, *Deathly Hallows*, 436.

INDEX